Owens

THE
FINANCIALLY INDEPENDENT WOMAN

Also by Barbara Lee

The Woman's Guide to the Stock Market
Take Control of Your Money

T H E
FINANCIALLY
INDEPENDENT
WOMAN

A STEP–BY–STEP GUIDE TO
SUCCESSFUL INVESTING

BARBARA LEE

A Birch Lane Press Book
Published by Carol Publishing Group

Thanks to my agent, Elizabeth Frost Knappman, New England Publishing Associates; my conscientious reader, Richard P. Beebe; and to my daughter, Stephanie

Copyright © 1996 Barbara Lee
All rights reserved. No part of this book may be reproduced in any form, except by a newspaper or magazine reviewer who wishes to quote brief passages in connection with a review.

A Birch Lane Press Book
Published by Carol Publishing Group
Birch Lane Press is a registered trademark of Carol Communications, Inc.

Editorial, sales and distribution, rights and permissions inquiries should be addressed to Carol Publishing Group, 120 Enterprise Avenue, Secaucus, N.J. 07094

In Canada: Canadian Manda Group, One Atlantic Avenue, Suite 105, Toronto, Ontario M6K 3E7

Carol Publishing Group books may be purchased in bulk at special discounts for sales promotion, fund-raising, or educational purposes. Special editions can be created to specifications. For details, contact: Special Sales Department, Carol Publishing Group, 120 Enterprise Avenue, Secaucus, N.J. 07094

Manufactured in the United States of America
10 9 8 7 6 5 4 3 2 1

Library of Congress Cataloging-in-Publication Data

Lee, Barbara, 1941–
    The financially independent woman : a step-by-step guide to
successful investing / Barbara Lee.
        p.   cm.—("A Birch Lane Press book.")
    Includes index.
    ISBN 1-55972-366-1
    1. Woman—Finance, Personal.   2. Investments.   3. Retirement—
Planning.   I. Title.   II. Series.
HG179.L416   1996
332.024′042—dc20   96-30271
                                                            CIP

Contents

Introduction   vii

Part I: Why

1. What Is Investing?   1
2. Why Should You Invest?   6
3. What Is Your Investment Dollar?   9
4. Setting Your Own Investment Goals   17
5. Defining Your Risk-Tolerance   20

Part II: With What

6. Low-Risk Investment Tools   26
7. Medium-Risk Investment Tools   33
8. High-Risk Investment Tools   41
9. Speculative Investment Tools   49

Part III: Where

10. Working With a Stockbroker   58
11. Working With a Bank   68
12. Working With Mutual Funds   71
13. Investing Through Retirement Plans   85
14. Investing Through Tax-Deferred Annuities   96

Part IV: When

15.	Ages Twenty-Five to Thirty-Nine	103
16.	Ages Forty to Fifty-Four	114
17.	Ages Fifty-Five and Up	131

Part V: How

18.	What to Read and Watch	147
19.	Do Not Make These Investment Mistakes!	155
20.	Do Follow These Investing Principles	159
	Conclusion	162
	Index	164

Introduction

Congratulations! Even though you are more than aware that you are already overburdened with the stresses of work life, home life, lack of free time to exercise, play, think, or just do nothing, you are willing to stretch a little more and commit some of that precious time to thinking about money and investing.

This commitment is as important as any other you will ever make in your life. There is no time in your life when you should not be thinking about money management. It is never too early to begin to think about increasing your own net worth. Equally important, it is never too late to make the plan which will give you financial security and knowledge.

Women have moved out of the house and have become wage earners. Many of us are no longer housewives. Although the traditional fields of nursing, secretarial worker, and teaching are still viable career paths, we also see women in new roles as welders, electricians, computer programmers, and trial lawyers. We are now bringing home our own paychecks. We owe it not only to ourselves but also to those we love to manage our funds wisely.

Men are not programmed to drop their paychecks in our hands these days. Today's woman is not the married woman of yesteryear whose job it was to pay the bills and keep the checkbook in balance. The expenses of yesterday had not begun to accelerate to where they are today. A college education, not to mention graduate school, was neither anticipated nor required. The years following retirement were not years that one might think about looking forward to and planning for.

Today's woman might not even be married. She is just as

likely to be single, divorced, or widowed.

Today's woman is defined by her own tax bracket. She may have her own discretionary income. She might be making a salary or receiving alimony. She might be expecting an inheritance or, to the contrary, worrying about how she will support her own elderly parents. Today's woman faces today's financial dilemmas.

It is no longer enough simply to rejoice in the fact that you're a woman out there earning your own money. There is still nothing to celebrate until you know what it means to control your own finances and financial destiny.

Money is an integral part of your life. Money should be used to make more money for you. It should also be used to make your life better. No more passing the buck and saying you have what you have only after the IRS, American Express, Visa, your local bank, and your favorite department store take their chunks. Now is the time to start to learn how to put yourself in charge of your own financial world.

By the time you finish this book, you will know not only what questions to ask of a financial adviser, you will know many of the answers yourself. You will understand what your own assets are and you will be ready to determine how best these assets should work for you.

This book will teach you *how* to think about money. You will learn to factor in your risk-tolerance before making an investment decision. You will become familiar with the many investment opportunities available to you. No matter what your age or experience, this book will show you exactly *where* your money should go—and *when*—to do the best job for you.

1

What Is Investing?

INVESTING IS USING MONEY for the primary purpose of making more money. Investing is also using money to boost income or to increase capital. Every person who has ever made an investment does so for one or more of the above reasons.

These reasons have existed from the beginning of time. It is both interesting and amusing to look up the word *invest* in a fifty-year-old dictionary or thesaurus. I found adages as old-fashioned as "to feather one's nest," admonitions such as "to guard against," and definitions as enduring as "save to fall back upon" or "prepare and provide for."

You'll note that none of these phrases even hint that there's anything to be gained by keeping your money under the mattress or burying it in a pot in the backyard. Hidden money doesn't earn interest. Entombed money doesn't work for you. Investors hundreds of years ago knew that. The need for investing has existed since the stone age. Only the tools, the materials, and the mechanisms have changed over the centuries.

Money matters currently seem to come into focus for most women twice a year: December and April.

In December you realize the fiscal and calendar year is drawing to a close. Before the new year, you might make a pass at trying to get your financial affairs in order.

Come April 15, you have to pay the Internal Revenue Service—and perhaps pay even more than you had anticipated because you did not take the time to plan properly. On the other hand, you might have the good fortune to be one up on Uncle Sam. You may be one of those fortunate enough to be the recipient of a refund. You have in your hand a check you could put to work for you. You have a gift from the IRS but, sadly, the odds are that this refund will get lost in your checking account. I want to convince you not to let the investment urge fade away.

Investing is a year-round program, not a twice-a-year frightening specter. The other ten months are wrongly neglected. I am not saying that there are not steps that can be taken at year-end, but emergency recourses are not part of sound money management. Regular investing is the only form of efficient investing. An hour spent once a month can eliminate this twice-per-year hand wringing.

We are all too familiar with the discipline needed to stay on a diet or to be faithful to an exercise regimen. The cheating dieter regains the weight. The weekend athlete risks possible injury in the pursuit of a Saturday sweat. The undisciplined investor faces an even worse scenario: lost money. Losing money is a lot more serious than extra poundage or a spare tire around the waist.

Grace M. called me at her son's suggestion in a puzzled panic recently. She told me she is a fifty-three-year-old divorcée with two grown children, a paid-up mortgage, $50,000 in mutual funds which she still does not understand, and the sole beneficiary of her still living parents' wills.

"My bank's apparently been sending me notices that my account is overdrawn," she said, "but I never bother to open those envelopes. I still wouldn't know except that I just received a phone call from a vice president to tell me my account's going to be closed unless I make an immediate deposit."

"Haven't you been keeping track of your money?" I asked.

"I didn't think I had to," she answered. "I mean it's not like I write checks for expensive items like fur coats or new cars. I just buy my groceries, pay for my dry cleaning, buy some cosmetics. You know. I deposit my paycheck and assume it'll cover my expenses. I guess I never paid enough attention to where all the money goes."

It is one thing to rationalize that your scale is out of kilter. It is a completely different story when your bank or brokerage account becomes unbalanced or out of sync. Although Grace's situation may be an extreme one, it still is all too easy to try to ignore what you do not understand.

Ever since the stock market crash of October 1987, Wall Street and the stock market in particular have been headline news more than at any other time in recent history. Greed governed most investment decisions pre-crash, but greed alone cannot be blamed for those disastrous few days. What can be blamed, though, is the perception by the public that it was so easy to make money.

Just as we all know that there is no such thing as a free lunch, there is no time when a stock's only direction is north, as we say in the business. When someone tells you you cannot lose, keep your hands in your pocket. Probably the only thing that can happen is that you will lose!

In those mid-October days, the public was willing to let itself be conned into believing that the market had no place to go but up. This same public learned to its vast dismay that what goes up comes down even faster.

For too many women, fear today has replaced greed as the prevalent market emotion. These women remember the crash and the plummeting of their net worth. Fear is keeping them still paralyzed on the sidelines. When you let yourself be ruled by fear, your finances suffer the same debilitating outcome as they would if you were enticed by greed.

The unavoidable paradox is that money is a fact of life. You need money to fund your lifestyle. It is only through investing that these money needs can be met. College tuitions did not decrease just because the stock market tumbled. Food, transportation, and entertainment costs do not recede in tandem with a lessening of the value of your stock and bond portfolio. Your bank officer does not care if the dollar is falling in value vis-à-vis the yen when your loan interest is due.

I will talk throughout this book about various strategies you can use at different times of your life depending on your life situation as well as the economic environment. I will always tell you the risk involved in these strategies.

Investing does not have to involve esoteric computer programs or a sophisticated understanding of higher mathematics. What is important is that you understand from the start that even the purchase of a savings E bond for your children or grandchildren counts as a form of investing. Moving money from a noninterest-bearing checking account into a savings or money market account means you are forcing your money to work a little bit harder for you.

By starting to think about your money earlier rather than later, you can get a jump start on concentrating on your own investment goals. Investing can cover immediate needs as well as long-term ones. You invest to try to make today and tomorrow as secure and comfortable for yourself and your family as possible.

The key is thinking and planning. I am going to take you by the hand and lead you through the investment arena. What you may now think of as a maze will soon become an easy-to-decipher map.

Investing is not a game of darts. A little bit of luck and timing never hurt any of us, but remember that get-rich-quick schemes are just that: schemes. Do not enter the stock market arena hoping to make a significant killing. Do not go to sleep hallucinating that you are going to become wealthy overnight.

It is definitely more sensible, and, ultimately, more profitable to invest with the fable of the tortoise and the hare in mind. The hare hit the ground running, but the tortoise slowly, yet confidently, won the race.

The successful investor does not need to predict interest-rate directions infallibly. It may be a challenge to outsmart the guest on "Wall Street Week," but it is not a challenge that must be met to guarantee your own investing prowess.

Buy stock in a company because you believe in the fundamental value of that company. Buy stock because you like the way management is running the company.

Investing begins with taking the time necessary to figure out what you want your investments to do for you. Then you will determine how much time you will allot them to accomplish your investment goals.

In summary, investing means using your money, by means of a planned program, for the dual purposes of earning interest and securing profits for yourself.

Every woman should always be investing. She should be investing in an organized way within a well-thought-out program. I hope by reading this book you will start to build your own investment house. Today you will begin to think about investing and start to plan the creation of that house. You are going to begin investing as systematically as you do everything else in your day.

2

Why Should You Invest?

MONEY NEEDS ARE AS COMPELLING as any other desire you will ever have in life. Is there any one of us who hasn't fantasized about winning the lottery? How many times have you played keno certain this time that you had the right combination of numbers? Easy riches are something we all desire. They are something we all envy as well. But money-come-easy is not part of the real word of finance.

The good news is that reality often comes about because of the dreams that we carry within us. We can make something happen because we envision it or, simply, because we need it. Our wishes can be strong enough to propel us to try to realize them. In that sense, it is not only legitimate, but also necessary, to have financial dreams and wishes.

Financial aspirations can and will be achieved with proper investing. You know you want to make money. You know you want to make your money work better for you. Investing is the best possible way to maximize that money.

Investing is a personal matter. Your choice of investments will be tailored to an individualized framework that fits only you. I will show you in detail in a later chapter how to draw up your own plan. For now, I only want to emphasize that there is no one investing program that works for every woman. Each plan becomes a unique one because you, alone, will input both the money and time.

A main reason to invest is to avoid financial standstill—or

even worse, financial reverse! Sometimes the demands of daily life are overwhelming enough that money planning becomes a matter of perennial contemplation. Procrastination replaces doing. The excuses for avoiding planning are infinite: job pressures, children, husband, inflation, recession, post-election jitters, pre-election jitters, volatile markets, fear of fees and expenses, and so on. You see the pattern.

These excuses are the same reasons you *should be* investing. For instance, you want to know where to put your money in inflationary or recessionary times. You want to know what to do in both high and lower interest rate times.

The doing is not really such a daunting task. Devote one evening to discarding your financial inertia. Do not let your funds sink into a quagmire without at least putting up a fight.

Sometimes the interest rate is so high that it would be foolhardy not to take advantage of such risk-free investments as money market accounts. But in low interest-rate times, you would invest instead in growth situations. An increase in your net worth must compensate for the loss of current income.

Careful investing enables you to make money in a good or bad economy, in an up or down stock market and in a Democratic or Republican administration. You will also see from reading this book that investing is not synonymous with paying undue fees.

You invest to have your money create more wealth for you as expeditiously as possible during any and all economic scenarios. No one economic environment should be dreaded more than any other. The goal of judicious investing is to make sure that you know *where* you're going and *how* you intend to get there.

It does not matter in theory whether interest rates are in fact rising or falling, because you are prepared in either instance. It is not your concern if one of the more flamboyant market commentators trashes a stock you hold in your portfolio. Your portfolio's value will never be dependent upon any one stock or bond.

It may be of interest to you to know if the Nikkei average tanked overnight, if the Paris Bourse made new highs, or if the

Brazilian Bolsa started to stabilize. These directions are of an informational nature only and should not disturb your financial peace of mind. Your investing program is not one of the moment.

There is neither magic nor mystery in money management. There are no secret incantations or esoteric formulas. Financial dreams can and will be met with careful investing.

As one of my clients said to me recently: "I now have my Ph.D. I have a job and I have a house. I can finally save money—which means I can start investing for the long term. The only thing is, I don't know what I feel comfortable with in that whole big world of investments!"

Clearly, the first thing she and I needed to determine was what, precisely, was her investment money.

3

What Is Your Investment Dollar?

INVESTMENTS ARE MADE with investment money. Your investment dollar is not the same as your food dollar, rent dollar, entertainment, laundry, or gas dollar. Think of all your money as one great big pie. Each of the above items is a slice of this pie. The investment dollar is one of these slices. It should not be combined with any other.

By the time you are ready to start investing, you will know how large that slice is going to be. Although investment monies are liquid, you should mentally set yourself against withdrawing that money except for an emergency. You may not be able to add to this money as regularly as you would like to, but try to leave it there so it can continue to work for you.

It's now time to do the work necessary to identify exactly what your investment money is. First we have to create a personal financial profile. Using this profile, we can then make a good estimate of your net worth.

Net worth, simply, is the difference between what you *own*—your assets—and what you *owe*—your liabilities. Knowing your net worth and understanding it is a major step toward financial self-confidence. Net worth is not a static number. It needs refiguring depending upon changes in your life. Have you switched jobs? Did you take a salary increase or decrease? Did

9

you get married? Divorced? Were you left an inheritance? Do you rent or did you just buy a home? Do you have a car or do you take public transportation? Did you make any switches in your retirement plans?

A realistic financial position cannot be quantified without an accurate portrayal of what you own and what you owe. You will need to know these figures in order to plan for the future disbursements of your funds.

The easiest way to discover exactly how and where you spend your money is to create a personal financial profile. The profile will take a little longer to draw up than a casual guestimate of your bank account activity. The time is worth it, however, because the profile, once constructed, will encompass all inflow, outflow, and net worth figures.

Ideally, you do not want your outflow to be more than your inflow for any time period. Sometimes, around tax time for instance, you may not be able to arrange things so systematically. It is essential, however, that you determine for yourself how much you need to live on and what funds come in to cover this amount.

The first worksheet to fill out is the one titled "Living Expenses." Your checking account statements for at least the past three months will give you most of the information you'll need to fill in the blanks.

You'll also need receipts and bill stubs for your big-ticket items (e.g., stereo equipment, computer). The three months don't necessarily have to be consecutive ones. In fact, a random choice of months representing different times of the year often gives a truer picture into seasonal spending patterns.

Holiday times are obvious drags on the budget. But you might also see, for instance, that gas and car maintenance payments rise in the summer, while food and entertainment costs rise instead in the winter.

You will need to record any investments you've made to date and any large ticket items you've purchased (e.g., stereo equipment, computer).

Living Expenses

	Monthly	Yearly
Housing:		
mortgage/rent	———	———
electricity	———	———
oil/gas	———	———
water	———	———
maintenance and repairs	———	———
telephone	———	———
household help	———	———
household supplies/products	———	———
Food:		
food purchased at work	———	———
groceries	———	———
liquor	———	———
eating out	———	———
miscellaneous	———	———
Clothing:		
clothing purchases	———	———
dry cleaning	———	———
laundry	———	———
other	———	———
Transportation:		
car payment	———	———
parking fees	———	———
commuting fares	———	———
public transportation	———	———
gas	———	———
maintenance and repairs	———	———
other	———	———
Medical:		
health insurance	———	———
doctor	———	———
dentist	———	———
other	———	———

medicine	_____	_____

Children:
child-care expense	_____	_____
tuition	_____	_____
private lessons	_____	_____
clothing	_____	_____
miscellaneous	_____	_____

Other expenses:
vacations	_____	_____
entertainment	_____	_____
gifts	_____	_____
pets/pet care	_____	_____
major purchases	_____	_____
miscellaneous	_____	_____

Totals:	_____	_____

The next worksheet will itemize your assets. You own your assets.

Assets

Annual salaries and wages	_____

Other income:
interest	_____
dividends	_____
alimony	_____
child support	_____
Deferred compensation	_____
Self-employment income	_____
Tax refunds	_____

Cash in bank accounts:
checking	_____
savings	_____

Cash in money market account funds   _____
Credit union account   _____
Market value of securities you hold:
   stocks   _____
   bonds   _____
   certificates of deposit   _____
   Treasury bills   _____
Market value of retirement accounts:
   IRA   _____
   Keogh   _____
   401(k)   _____
Amount vested in company pension plan   _____
Value of stock in company stock purchase plan _____
Present value of your home, if you own it
   (have recent appraisal done)   _____
Cash value of any life insurance policies   _____
Cash value of annuities   _____
Personal belongings
   (have recent appraisal done):
   art   _____
   antiques   _____
   collectibles   _____
   jewelry   _____
Home entertainment electronics   _____
Personal computer   _____
Value of cars owned (consult dealer's
Blue Book):   _____
   motorcycle   _____
   boat   _____
Money owed to you   _____

Total Assets: _____

The third and last worksheet you will need to complete is the
one itemizing your liabilities. A liability is money that you owe.

Liabilities

Annual taxes:
  real estate   _____
  federal personal income tax (estimate
    based on previous year's return)   _____
  state and local income tax   _____
  personal property   _____
Mortgage   _____
Insurance premiums:
  home   _____
  personal liability   _____
  household   _____
  car   _____
  fine arts and valuables   _____
Insurance policy loans   _____
Personal debts   _____
Loans:
  credit card   _____
  car   _____
  department store charges   _____
  school   _____
Margin account debit balance   _____
Charitable pledges and contributions _____

Total Liabilities: _____

The most aggravating part of the exercise is now completed—unless, in a worst case scenario, you see a vast discrepancy figure favoring your liabilities over your assets. If that is true, you are not ready to invest. You have no investment money available. Your first task is to pay off your debts and get on an even financial kilter.

Let us examine your total assets versus your total liabilities more closely. These two portions of your profile tell us a story. These numbers help you establish your overall financial picture. They show you the results of your money management—or your lack thereof. You can tell at a glance whether you are living within your means, beyond your means, or just treading water.

What you want to see is that the asset total is more than the liability total. If the opposite is true, but not overwhelmingly so, don't panic. Even though the numbers indicate that you are getting poorer, and not richer, this fact is not an irrevocable one. There is no such thing as financial destiny. You have the power to change your course.

A major benefit to completing this exercise is being able to see *precisely* where these liabilities are outweighing your assets. You may be able to start a program of financial readjustment yourself simply by knowing where, for example, you are spending more than you are taking in. You can quickly tell if you are borrowing more than you are making. Remember, you are not ready to start an investment program until your assets are, at minimum, equal to your liabilities. The investment dollar cannot be created until this balance is achieved.

In the majority of cases, you will find from doing the math that the bottom line number is a pleasing one. You have a positive net worth figure. (Your net worth figure is reached by subtracting your total liabilities from your total assets.) You have actually been saving more than you realized. You do have money to invest—money which you want to use to make that net worth even greater.

But we are not quite at the finish line. We still need to quantify the size of that slice of the pie. This is where the total reached on your "Living Expenses" worksheet becomes significant. Subtract this total from your total *annual income*, reached by adding together your annual salary, other income, and all available cash itemized on the "Assets" worksheet. The resulting amount is the amount available to be used as your investment dollar.

Lastly, you must now add this newly created category to your "Living Expenses" worksheet. This new figure will now be part of your calculations the next time you redo your personal financial profile. Over time, the numbers themselves will verify for you whether you are, or are not, financially qualified to increase your investment money amount.

In summary, knowing how much you have to invest is an essential piece of information. Money set aside for investment purposes can only be identified after you have earmarked other monies for all your daily and yearly expenses and emergencies. You yourself define this amount by creating your own financial profile.

As I stated at the beginning of this chapter, the amount that you allocate for investment is not what is important. What is important is that this particular slice exists in the first place. You cannot invest until specific money is identified as your investment dollar.

The next task is to learn how to fit that dollar into your own customized investment plan.

4

Setting Your Own Investment Goals

FINANCIAL SKILL IS NOT GENDER-ORIENTED. It is no more a masculine talent than it is a feminine one. It is a skill which we all need to cultivate in today's economic environment.

Successful investing also should not take undue time. What it does take, as I have already mentioned several times, is planning. And planning means setting financial goals for yourself.

These goals are individual ones. They belong only to you. They are not tidbits for cocktail conversation. Nor should you have to defend them to anyone else. In fact, from studies conducted regarding the emotional meaning of money, it has been shown that women are much more likely to talk about their job troubles, marital difficulties, or even menopausal problems than they are to mention anything about their incomes.

Your own objectives and your own financial resources are unique to you. The answers to your financial needs will be unique to you as well.

In setting your goals, it as important for you take into account your emotional requirements as well as your monetary ones. For instance, Anne, a thirty-eight-year-old, unmarried account executive at a major advertising agency, has the money to justify a growth-oriented investment stance. When we talked, however, she became visibly nervous at the thought of not being assured of a fixed return on her investments. It was clearly better for her to stick to conservative investments and be able to sleep at night.

You must define your goals before you can draw up your own individual plan. Typical goals include the following:

- create more financial security for yourself (and your family)
- purchase a second (vacation) home
- bolster monthly cash flow to meet daily living needs
- increase net worth: see assets grow
- hedge versus inflation
- protect against long-term illness or disability
- meet retirement needs
- minimize taxes

Because financial needs are in constant motion, your plan must be similarly flexible. It is impossible to sit down at the age of thirty, forty, or even fifty, and map out an ironclad plan of investment for the rest of your life. Opportunities change. Values of investments change. Tax laws change.

One fact that never changes, no matter what the stage of your career, life situation, or age, is the necessity of knowing where you stand financially. You must be ready to set and reset financial goals as these different phases unfold.

Making your plan doesn't mean working overtime. A few hours—once you've completed the above worksheets—should be more than sufficient. And the good news is that once the plan is done, it is done. An annual review should be enough to factor in any of the necessary changes in your life.

In order for your plan to work as expeditiously as possible, I will make one recommendation and give one warning. The recommendation is that you will be helping your own financial future if you can make regular contributions to your investment money over a specified period of time. The amount is not important. Making the disciplined contribution is what counts.

There may be times you find you simply cannot add to that

slice of the pie. That's all right. But what I really caution against, barring a true emergency, is taking away from this piece. You are hurting both your own investment program as well as your financial adviser by taking unplanned withdrawals.

I had been very successful with Phylis's portfolio a couple of months ago. I'd bought some bank stocks for her which had been takeover candidates and the takeovers occurred. Her $60,000 investment account was up 10 percent to $66,000 for the month. She called me overjoyed with her new equity figure. Then she called me back a week later and asked me to send her a check for $3,000.

Not only was my performance figure lessened, but, more importantly, so was Phylis's account value—an account that she had told me was her nest egg and all she knew she could count on for her retirement years.

The warning is that you must be patient. Investments and goals take time to work out. You must give yourself enough time for your plan to be fully implemented. The investment universe is not a static one. The stock market fluctuates each day and during the day.

Give your goals the appropriate time they need to be met. Wait out market fluctuations. Stick firmly to your own investment objectives.

More money is lost in the financial arena by investors not sticking to their own investment objectives than by any other means. Your plan and your goals fit only you. Only a change in finances dictates a change in plan.

As I indicated in Anne's case, earlier, your risk tolerance plays as much a part in defining your plan as your financial capabilities do. It is now time to talk about risk.

5

Defining Your Risk-Tolerance

RISK IS INHERENT in any monetary transaction even if you abdicate all decisions and hide your money under the mattress. Actually, the risk to your money in case of fire or theft is actually higher by this decision than it would be if you chose, instead, to put your money into a savings account in your bank or into a money market account at a brokerage firm.

The amount of risk in the investment area is relative depending upon the investment choice or choices. There is a wide spectrum between buying Treasury obligations, investing in blue chip stocks or trading oat futures in the commodity markets. Choosing between investments involves a conscious and deliberate trade-off between risk and return.

An economic truism is that the greater the risk, the greater the return. Some women cannot invest without receiving the commensurate thrill of the possibility of realizing a high return. Other women, however, suffer palpitations at the mere hint that some of their principal could be in jeopardy.

There is no right or wrong in your risk attitude. The investment truism doesn't relate to the no pain, no gain exercise theory. Investment should never include so much risk that the investing process itself becomes a painful one.

Ibbotson & Associates conducted a study of the risk/return

trade-off received in a one-year investment period during the years 1926 through 1991. In the low-risk category, Treasury bills in their best year rose 14 percent. There was 0 percent loss in the worst year.

The Standard & Poor's Index of 500 stocks rose 54 percent in its best year and declined 43 percent in its worst. The most aggressive investment, small stocks, rose 143 percent in their best year, but also fell 58 percent in the worst case. As the saying goes, if you want to play, you've often got to pay!

I am often asked by first-time women investors, "How can I select the right investment at the right time?" One part of the answer is to be well informed about the investment vehicles available to you. I will be talking about these specific vehicles in the next section, but being aware of your risk-tolerance is an equally important factor in making your selections.

A portfolio should also never be an entirely risk-oriented one—no matter what your financial or emotional strengths. Diversification not only between investments but also between risk levels is necessary for overall portfolio performance. There are even times due to economic or political events that you might be better off sidestepping the market and sitting on the sidelines in liquid investments such as money markets or Treasury bills.

Conversely, in my twenty years as a stockbroker, I have seen many times a woman with the most conservative portfolio deciding to put a small amount into risk investments. This makes perfect sense to me if we have covered all her financial goals and needs with the bulk of her portfolio. Designating a discrete amount, 5 to 10 percent at most, out of your investment monies to be used aggressively can give you the reward potential as well as be fun!

Oddly enough, in my experience, it is usually the older retired or widowed client who chooses this adventuresome path. Since successful risk-investing calls for speed, attention to timing, and the ability to cut losses when necessary, I usually ask these clients for discretion on these trades. Discretion means that I buy or sell at will without having to call the client for explanations or approval before conducting the trade. The client, however, is still fully informed and receives the same confirmation slip that she receives on trades where I do not exercise discretion.

The risk involved in many investment choices is clear-cut. Commodity trading, hedging, and option buy and selling are probably all familiar terms—terms that may give some of you shivers. I am not trying to persuade you to cast aside your fear and jump into these waters. I want you to understand the risk spectrum, especially in the less obvious categories, and be able to make your own educated choices.

Moody's and Standard & Poor's are two well-known organizations that rate the creditworthiness of bonds. Their designations vary slightly but generally range from a triple-A rating, through the Bs and Cs, all the way down to D. AAA, for example, means best quality. BBB indicates medium quality, and a D tells you the bond is in default.

Standard & Poor's also rates stocks, but you are better off looking at the rating assigned to the particular stock by the brokerage firm you are using. Each firm has its own system, but I'll use my firm's system to illustrate. My firm has both a number and letter designation for rating each stock it follows. The number indicates the stock analyst's judgment for the expected price performance of the stock relative to the Standard & Poor's 500 in the coming year to year and a half.

The numbers range from one (1) to five (5) with 1 being a buy, 3 being neutral, and 5 meaning a sell.

The letter rating indicates the risk factor. The letters are L (low risk), M (medium risk), H (high risk), and S (speculative).

Again, let me emphasize two points. Risk is not a pejorative term. It is an element of investing that you must be aware of. Second, this rating system is my firm's. Other brokerage firms will have their own rating system. Also, the same stock will often receive different ratings at different firms depending upon what that firm's analyst believes.

Lastly, if you are thinking of investing in a mutual fund, look toward a big player name that has what is called a "family" of funds. Within each family there will be differentiations articulated as to both the objectives and goals of each particular fund.

The following quiz will help you identify what type of investments fit both your financial and emotional risk tolerance.

Investment and Risk Quiz

Choose the answer which most closely pertains to you. In the column at the far right, insert the number in parentheses which corresponds to your answer.

My age is closest to:
(9) 35   (7) 45   (5) 55   (3) 65   (1) 75   _____

My total annual income (salary, alimony, dividends, interest etc.) from all sources is nearest to (in thousands):
(2) $20   (4) $35   (5) $50   (6) $75   (8) $100+   _____

In comparison to my income, my annual expenses approximate:
(1) 100%   (3) 90%   (5) 80%   (7) 70%   (9) 50%   _____

I claim this many dependents:
(9) 0   (8) 1   (6) 2–3   (4) 4–5   (1) 6+   _____

My assets total in thousands (refer back to worksheet):
(1) $50   (3) $100   (5) $200   (7) $300   (9) $500+   _____

My liabilities are what percentage of my assets (use worksheet numbers):
(9) 30%   (7) 50%   (5) 75%   (3) 90%   (1) 100%   _____

I have cash or liquid assets readily available to meet the expenses for what period of time:
(1) 1 month (3) 2 months (5) 3 months (7) 4 months
(9) 6+ months   _____

My health insurance coverage includes:
(9) basic, major medical, catastrophic, long-term disability, dental
(7) basic, major medical, dental
(5) basic, major medical
(1) basic

I have some kind of retirement plan:
(9) 401(k) or 403(b); vesting where I work; or participation in a defined benefit or defined contribution plan
(5) Keogh or SEP
(3) IRA
(0) No plan

Add up your total score and divide by nine. Match that number with the number of the following list of investment possibilities. The lower the number, the lower the risk. You do not *have* to invest in the highest number you can afford financially. The quiz is a only a guideline. The investments on any particular level may legitimately exceed your risk threshold. Step down a few levels then and reexamine your alternatives.

1. insured certificates of deposit or government money market accounts; passbook accounts
2. U.S. Government bonds
3. high-quality corporate or tax-free bonds, preferred stocks, deferred annuities
4. lower-rated taxable or tax-free bonds, mortgage-backed bonds, higher-rated bond mutual funds, convertible bonds
5. higher-rated common stocks and stock mutual funds
6. lower-rated common stocks and stock mutual funds
7. speculative high-yield bonds, aggressive growth stocks, global investments
8. metals, gold and silver, emerging growth stocks and funds, biotech, cyberspace, real estate
9. rarities and exotic tangibles: art, antiques, stamps, first editions, gemstones

Do not be dismayed if right now you cannot handle the risk profile your net worth supposedly tells you that you should handle. Women as a general rule are less risk-tolerant than men. This does not mean your portfolio will not work as well as a man's. In fact, under certain market and interest-rate conditions, the less risky your portfolio, the better the performance. The risk decision is yours and yours alone. Your financial adviser is the only other person who can help you arrive at the right level of risk for you.

Before you can begin to narrow down your investment choices, however, it is time to learn what is out there and what each investment vehicle can accomplish for you.

PART II: WITH WHAT

6

Low-Risk Investment Tools

LOW-RISK INVESTMENT TOOLS are a mandatory part of every woman's portfolio, whether she is a first-time investor or a long-time one. Low-risk investments are precisely where you should keep your three-or-so-month emergency fund—the amount that *every* investor should keep aside. As your experience and time in the market increases, you will probably choose to redeploy some of this money into higher-risk categories. Some of your money, however, must always remain at this level. Besides providing financial security, your low-risk money gives you cash that can be available for an unexpected financial emergency.

A low-risk investment is one that emphasizes safety of principal and a guaranteed return. A low-risk investment is purely income-oriented. The goal is preservation of capital—of keeping whatever assets you have stable while generating the maximum income stream.

There are several options available to you to maximize your current return even within this very basic level. One of the most obvious, but most often overlooked, is the money in your savings account or even in your interest-bearing checking account.

Yvonne opened an IRA with me several years ago when she was working as a bookkeeper for a free-lance photographer. She subsequently got a job with a major accounting firm with a corporate pension program so she no longer contributed to the IRA. The original IRA investment continued to perform well and there wasn't a need for us to be in regular touch.

Yvonne called me recently, however, to inform me that she had been able to save some extra money. She was interested in opening a stock brokerage account that had check-writing privileges. We discussed the financial requirements. Ten thousand dollars was the minimum amount required—and still is— to open such an account. Yvonne hadn't saved that much money yet but felt she'd be able to accumulate it in about six more months.

"Where are you keeping this money now?" I asked her.

"In my savings account," she answered.

"Do you know what interest rate you're getting?"

She told me to hold on. She had her bank statement right with her.

"It looks like two and three-quarters percent," she said. "That doesn't sound very good, does it? But I don't dare lose any of it, so I better keep it just where it is."

Yvonne didn't need to keep this money in a very low-interest-bearing account just to avoid any risk. By moving her funds from a savings account into a money market account, she could virtually double her return without increasing her risk exposure. Her principal amount would remain secure while the approximately 5 percent return she would earn in a money market would help her reach her financial goal that much sooner.

Yvonne's case isn't a singular one. First-time investors need to know that for even the most elementary investments, there can be more than one choice.

There are four main choices for investment at the no-risk level:

- savings accounts
- money market accounts
- certificates of deposit
- United States Treasury bills.

Let's take a close look at each one of these.

Passbook Savings Accounts

I'm going to lump together a passbook (or statement) savings account and an interest-bearing checking account. In most cases, this type of account will pay you as little as the bank can get away with paying you! And they are much faster at reducing them than they are at increasing them.

It may be true that a bank reevaluates the interest rate each week, but I assure you no bank raises its rate until the competition does. For this type of account, the banks are watching each other more than they are watching out for you.

The only benefit that comes immediately to mind is that there is no minimum balance necessary for this type of account. Also, your principal is safe even though the compounding interest—especially in relatively low interest times such as we are in now—doesn't amount to much each month. If you don't have the minimum amount necessary to open a money market account or if you are using this account only as a resting place for a few weeks, I would agree that the financial stamina necessary to move around funds probably is not worth it.

Money Market Accounts

Money market accounts usually have a minimum opening amount. These amounts have lessened over the years. By making a few phone calls, you should be able to find a bank, a brokerage firm, or a mutual fund that will open this type of account for as little as $1,500 to $2,500. This is often only an initial amount. You may be able to draw the balance below the minimum and still keep the account open. I couldn't allow a client to do this, but a friend of mine has great pride in a money market account she has with another retail brokerage firm where she maintains a $1.50 balance. The account remains open if needed.

Money market accounts are short-term money funds that the bank invests only in short-term debt securities. Money market funds are sold in shares of $1 apiece.

A money market resembles a savings account in that interest and dividends accrue daily. The difference is that the interest in a money market is pegged directly to other short-term debt instruments. If interest rates are climbing, that effect will be reflected in the fund almost immediately. There is little lag time. Conversely, if interest rates are falling, so will the yield on the money market fund.

The type of short-term instruments a money market fund invests in are ones targeted to large institutions that have the monetary resources necessary to purchase short-term instruments such as commercial paper. Commercial paper is a corporate bond representing very short-term loans to a company. Another example is a banker's acceptance note which is a commercial draft, somewhat like a promissory note to a bank, due at face value between one and nine months. More common investments would be short-term loans to municipalities, to government agencies, and thirty- to ninety-day Treasury bills.

All of the above are safe, high-quality interest-bearing instruments. What is not safe is a money market that promises you yields markedly above the others. It is always tempting to seek out the highest yield possible, but like the old adage says, if it sounds too good to be true, it surely is. Obviously there are higher-risk, lower-rated debt instruments available to institutions as well. You just don't want to be an investor in those particular money market funds.

Your low-risk money is there to be used in case of emergency. Emergency means being laid off from your job, becoming ill, your husband losing his job, your apartment losing its rent-controlled status. You need immediate money to cover you for these contingencies. You certainly don't need the money itself creating another emergency for you.

Certificates of Deposit (CDs)

A certificate of deposit differs primarily from a money market account in that you are giving up a certain amount of instant liquidity for possibly a slightly higher return.

A CD is a time deposit which gives you a specified interest rate over a stated period of time. CDs are issued in varying maturities ranging from thirty days to ten years. The longer the maturity, the less the liquidity, and the higher the interest rate attached.

State as well as national banks issue their own certificates of deposit. So do trust companies and state or federal savings and loans. A CD is a direct obligation of the issuing institution. Brokerage firms and banks both act as placement agents for these CDs.

CDs are usually sold in denominations of $1,000 but often have $5,000 as the minimum purchase amount. Their interest rates are established weekly at noon on Monday (unless a holiday intervenes). These rates are fixed for the lifetime of the CD. A short-term certificate, for instance one due in three to six months, will pay interest only at maturity. A year certificate tends to pay semiannually. A longer-term CD might even pay monthly interest. There is almost always a penalty attached to this investment tool if you take an early withdrawal.

United States Treasury Bills

A U.S. Treasury bill that has the same maturity as a certificate of deposit will yield less than the CD, but it has a specific quality which may make the slightly lesser yield preferable. The interest on any Treasury obligation, a bill, a bond, or a note, is exempt from state and local tax. The interest is only taxable at the federal level. If you are in a higher tax bracket, or if you live in a state with a high state or city tax, it is very conceivable that you will actually take home more with the partially exempt Treasury interest than the fully taxable CD interest. This is true of New York and Massachusetts but not Florida and Texas.

The United States government has to borrow money the same way corporations and municipalities do. One way the government conducts this borrowing is to issue Treasury bonds, notes, and bills. Treasury bills are differentiated from bonds and notes by maturity length. T-bills, as they are called, are issued for lengths of three, six, or twelve months.

Notes cover a one- to ten-year period, and bonds are securities of longer than ten-year maturities. I will talk more about notes and bonds in the next chapter on medium-risk instruments.

T-bills do not have coupons (see the next chapter) because the bills are issued at a discount. You buy a Treasury bill at a discount price from par ($1,000). The difference in price between your purchase amount and $1,000 is the interest. This price is based on the prevailing level of interest rates. At the maturity date, the full value, or $1,000 per bill, will be paid to you.

Treasury bills are highly liquid. They may be cashed in any day, and you'll receive your money back on the next business day. There is no penalty for early redemption. You will receive whatever the market price is for the Treasury on that given day.

You can buy Treasuries in one of three ways:

1. directly from the Federal Reserve bank yourself
2. from your bank
3. from your brokerage firm.

Why would you choose one of the above over another?

The only real advantage to buying yourself from the Federal Reserve is that you will pay no service charge. The fee charged by a bank or a brokerage firm is approximately $60 for the transaction, no matter how many bills are bought.

The disadvantage in buying directly is that a bit more effort is involved and the no-service charge may not compensate for the time and effort involved. To purchase directly from the Fed, you must complete an order form and mail (or appear in person with) a check for the face amount of the bill desired.

Your bank or brokerage firm will simply take the order from you a few days before the weekly auction, purchase the bills for you and debit your bank or brokerage account.

It is also easier to sell before maturity if your securities are held at a brokerage firm or bank. The Federal Reserve will not take early redemptions. Therefore, if you have to sell all or a portion of a Treasury, you would have to open a bank or brokerage account and deposit the securities in that account. This takes time.

The minimum purchase amount of T-bills is $10,000. Additional amounts are in increments of $5,000. The same minimum and multiples apply whether you buy these instruments at the Federal Reserve or through a financial institution.

Treasuries are viewed by most women as the safest investment they can make. And they are not wrong. There is something reassuring—most days—about being able to invest in a security that is guaranteed by the full faith and credit of the U.S. government and that is liquid and has a competitive yield, especially if tax considerations are relevant.

To review, *low-risk* investments give you:

- safety of principal—principal fluctuations are avoided
- short-term maturities
- moderate yields
- some form of tax savings if you buy Treasury obligations
- liquidity—ready access to your funds.

What you give up:

- higher overall returns
- having your investments in place—because of the short term you will have to make frequent (re)investment decisions.

7

Medium-Risk Investment Tools

MOST WOMEN WILL CHOOSE the medium-risk investment category to house the bulk of their investment money. Medium risk covers the combined goals of 1) income stability, and 2) growth.

A lot of investment how-to books and articles suggest that you imagine the spectrum of investment tools and goals to resemble a pyramid shape. The base, the largest part, of the pyramid is your foundation money, your seed money—the low-risk category. As you move up the pyramid, your investment choices become more aggressive but you assign fewer dollars the higher up the pyramid you climb.

I am not knocking this image because in earlier years and articles I have used it as well. I don't think it fits the woman investor of today, however. For one thing, I don't think it is as necessary to have the largest percentage of your money in a no-risk category. There are plenty of opportunities to achieve some growth without incurring uncomfortable degrees of risk. I also think that the shape of a pyramid makes the investor feel she *must* have some money in the speculative tip area. Let us go back to the pie image as opposed to the pyramid one. I'd rather use the term "investment categories" instead of "levels" because the word *level* implies that if you don't reach the top, you have not accomplished your goal. That simply is not so in the investment world. Women today should have the greatest concentration of their money in this second category. If you do not have an element of growth in your investment plan, you cannot expect to build wealth. Wealth cannot build effectively by income alone.

The two basic investment tools used for medium-risk income and growth are stocks and bonds. Those are just the two parents. Stocks have a whole family of variations and so do bonds.

Bonds

A *bond* is a debt security. It is a loan contract. This means that when you buy a bond you are *loaning* money to someone at a specified interest rate for a specified period of time. Assuming you do not cash in your loan ahead of time, or the borrower does not pay back the loan ahead of time, at the maturity date, the expiration, you will receive your full principal amount back along with any remaining interest due.

There are two broad types of bonds: *taxable* and *tax-free*. A *taxable bond,* called a corporate bond, simply means you are loaning money to a public company or corporation.

A *tax-free bond,* or a municipal bond, is a bond issued by a governmental body either at the state or federal level. Municipal bond interest is exempt at the federal level. The interest is exempt at the state and local level as well if you buy a bond issued by the state in which you live. An out-of-state bond's interest will be taxable on your state return. If your tax bracket is above 30 percent, a municipal bond might be the better investment for you. There are bond mutual funds available with the same characteristics.

A sort of hybrid bond is one issued by a government agency, such as the Treasury, discussed in the previous chapter or a bond issued by another agency, such as the Federal Farm Credit Bureau or the Federal Home Loan Bank. The interest from all of these types of government bonds is taxable at the federal level, but certain issues are exempt from state and local taxes.

Bonds are the senior issue, which means that because a bondholder is a creditor, she gets her money back first in case of bankruptcy or liquidation. Preferred stock shareholders come second, and common stock owners come last.

All bonds have a matured face value of $1,000. But bonds do not trade constantly at the same price. Many retired women—and women who come in with their husbands as well—have said to me they only want bonds in their portfolios because they do not want to see their principal vary in price. There can be every assurance that a decent rated bond will mature at $1,000, but it is also a fact that any bond's price will move below (and above) that price during its lifetime. Again, though, the lesser the amount of risk, the lesser the amount of fluctuation or volatility.

Three factors determine a bond's risk or lack thereof: its credit rating, the coupon, and the length to maturity.

Moody's and Standard & Poor's are the two best-regarded rating firms in the financial community. Moody's top rating is designated by "Aaa" while Standard & Poor's capitalizes its triple A (AAA). In this medium-risk category, you should stick to a bond with a single A rating or better.

The *coupon* is the stated interest rate the bond is going to pay you. This rate is part of a bond description. If you see a rate that is out of sync with current interest rates, you know you are looking at a riskier bond. A lower-regarded company is trying to entice you to lend it money by paying you a higher rate of return for the use of your money.

A medium-risk bond will not have a distant maturity date. I'd consider the appropriate time frame to be between one and seven years. I personally don't like to buy bonds much farther out than that for two reasons: I don't like to have my own money be somewhat illiquid for that long, and my own stomach couldn't handle the price fluctuations inherent in the long-term bond. I would willingly give up the possibility of getting a point or more higher in terms of coupon rate for the certainty that my money is going to come due at shorter time intervals.

Let's look at an actual bond listing in the newspaper. You'll be amazed at how much you can learn from the few letters and numbers in the listing.

Go to the New York bonds heading in the Business section of your newspaper. You'll see the second bond listed exactly like this: AMR 6-1/8 24.

There is a whole story here which I will unravel for you.

AMR stands for the parent company of what we used to know as American Airlines

The coupon is 6-1/8. This particular bond will pay you 6-1/8 percent interest twice a year for each bond you buy.

Finally, 24 means the bond will come due in 2024. This is a very long-term bond and for that reason this bond wouldn't qualify as a medium-risk investment.

All bonds, whether they are taxable or tax-free, have credit ratings, a stated coupon rate and a fixed maturity date. Some bonds, however, have a call feature attached to them. The call date is a set one, as is the call price. A company, or a municipality, would want to call in its bonds early if the prevailing interest rates have declined appreciably below the bond's coupon rates. It would be cheaper for the issuer to pay off its borrowers and reissue new bonds carrying a lower interest rate.

Bonds usually are bought with a minimum purchase of $10,000 and in increments of $5,000 above that. Occasionally, smaller pieces may be found, but if these amounts are more than you feel comfortable putting into any one single issue, I would recommend a mutual fund of either corporate or municipal bonds. I will talk in greater detail about mutual funds in a later chapter but, as a quick definition, a mutual fund is a large pool of bonds (or stocks) which are invested with a common goal or theme. Shares in a mutual fund can be purchased at much lower dollar amounts than individual bonds. You are not locked into your purchase. The shares may be redeemed, or sold, easily.

There are tax-free mutual funds available which tell you that all the bonds within the pool are of shorter maturities. Specific examples include the Fidelity Limited Term Municipals, Dreyfus

Intermediate Municipal Bond, and Vanguard Municipal Bond Fund Intermediate.

Another tool, which I will discuss fully in chapter 13 dealing with IRAs and college tuition, is the *zero coupon bond.* Because this type of bond carries very little risk, I need to include it in this category. A zero coupon means exactly that. While a traditional bond has a stated rate of interest and pays that interest semiannually, a zero coupon vehicle pays no interest.

The hook to the zero coupon instrument is that it is purchased at a discount to the maturity price. Similar to a series E bond, or a Treasury bill, the price of the zero moves toward par, or $1,000, over the lifetime of the investment. Interest, instead of being paid out, is automatically added to principal. Starting with the moment of investment, your money starts to grow toward its maturity value.

The amount of the discount depends upon the length of time until maturity. The longer the life of the bond, the deeper the discount. Zero coupons are issued on CDs, municipal and corporate bonds, and Treasury obligations.

Preferred Stocks

Preferred stocks rank senior to common stocks in a case of liquidation or bankruptcy. They have characteristics of both bonds and stocks. Preferreds resemble bonds in that they carry a stated dividend rate and sometimes have a mandatory call or expiration date. A preferred stock shareholder hasn't loaned the company money, however. Preferreds resemble common stocks in that they represent ownership in a company.

Preferreds pay dividends quarterly, as do other stocks, and not semiannually as do bonds. Because the preferred has a designated interest rate, this dividend acts as a cushion and protects it against some of the fluctuations the common stock of the same company might undergo.

An element of some preferred stocks is their convertible

feature. Convertible preferreds permit the stockholder to convert the preferred into common stock (at a set price) of the same. This means that the preferred holder has a chance to have her shares increase in price in relation to the movement of the common stock. Another feature to look for in a preferred is the cumulative advantage. This means that if a stock is a cumulative preferred, and the company misses one or more dividend payments, the preferred stockholder must receive her share of all the missed payments before the common stockholders receive any dividends.

Common Stock

The other major component of medium-risk investing is *common stock*. A stock is the exact opposite of a bond. A bondholder has loaned the company money. A stockholder is a part owner of that company—no matter how minuscule that ownership is relative to the whole. Each stock certificate represents evidence of ownership.

Stockholders have the right to vote on company matters. As a stockholder, you are invited to the annual meeting or you may vote by proxy. All shareholders must be informed about corporate profits, losses, sales, future prospects, etcetera.

If a company does not want to reveal these facts and does not want to be subject to outside voting of shareholders, it stays private. A private company has no reporting rules and regulations. Its stock is not traded on an exchange and outsiders cannot buy in.

As a stockholder, you benefit directly from the profits of your investment. As the company grows, the value of your investment grows as well either by increases in the amount of the dividend or by upward stock movement—or both!

Stocks in the medium-risk category should carry the potential of double return. A double return means that you are receiving a dividend yield from the stock of at least 4 percent, but you expect some growth from the stock as well. A pure income stock aims specifically for high dividends and would be purchased by someone as an alternative to a bond.

Stocks are listed on one of three exchanges:

- the New York Stock Exchange (NYSE)
- the American Exchange (AMEX)
- *National Association of Securities Dealers Automated Quotron* (NASDAQ), formerly known as the over-the-counter market

During her first appointment with me, Alice insisted that she only wanted to buy stocks on the NYSE because those were the safest investments. This is a widespread misconception. The reporting and capitalization requirements made by the New York Stock Exchange may be more stringent than the other exchanges but for various reasons a company may simply choose not to change its listing. For example, as of today's writing, stocks like America Online, Microsoft, Intel, and many other high-tech companies just to name a few certainly meet any fitness test but still remain on the NASDAQ system.

The major difference between the exchanges is that there is a location, an address, for the NYSE and the AMEX. All NASDAQ trading is done electronically and is conducted on a bid-and-ask format rather than a last-trade price.

There are two other listings for stocks, the supplemental and the pink sheets. Both of these indicate stocks which may not have track records, might not publish quarterly or annual reports, have a limited number of shares outstanding, etcetera. Any of these stocks belong in the high-risk category.

Again, if you have qualms about putting all or some of your money into any one company, investing in a mutual fund that has income and growth or income and stability as its printed objective is your best alternative. There is no dearth of these kinds of funds. You just want to make sure you buy from a reputable fund manager. Fidelity, Putnam, Vanguard, and Twentieth Century are a few of the better-known names.

To recap *medium-risk* investments:
What you get:

- moderate yields and growth potential
- narrow range of principal value movement
- regular or varied income depending upon investment
- high credit quality.

What you give up:

- high degree of liquidity
- negligible risk of short-term investments.

Typical investment tools:

- five- to seven-year Treasury or government agency bond
- short- or intermediate-term tax-free bond fund
- zero coupon bond
- "A" rated or better corporate bond
- high-rated preferred stock
- stock giving you a double return of dividend yield and growth
- income and growth stock mutual fund.

8

High-Risk Investment Tools

LILA S. HAS BEEN A CLIENT OF MINE for close to fifteen years. Her story is a classic one that illustrates the progression that can take place in any woman's portfolio.

Lila made her first appointment with me to fulfill a vow she made to herself on her thirtieth birthday. She had promised herself she was going to begin her own investment program that year no matter how small the sum she had available to start. Lila was married to a successful attorney and they had two young children. She had worked for a large interior decorating firm before her marriage. Now that her children were in school, she wanted to resume her career—but she planned on operating out of her own home with her own individual clients.

Lila and her husband had worked out their own bargain when their first child was born. Lila had agreed to quit her job and stay home with the understanding that her husband would provide all the medical insurance for the family and, since he was the primary wage earner, he would be completely responsible for the children's tuition bills through college.

"Even though all my needs are taken care of for as far as I can see," she'd said to me, "I still want to be responsible for some of my own future. I don't like being dependent upon anyone. I don't see any problems in my life, but you never know."

Lila's debut investment was, of course, a low-risk one. She had $2,500 to invest. I suggested she start with a six-month certificate of deposit. This way she would see the value of compounded interest. Her money would be liquid again in a very short period of time, but she would get her first taste of not being able to dip into her investment slice.

Initially Lila was only able to add to her account in $500 increments. As the principal amount grew, we were able to diversify, however, into larger CDs and then into a two-year Treasury note. Lila's husband Robert had by now been made a partner at his law firm and, since they did file jointly, the tax savings on the Treasury on their state return was helpful.

As her children grew, so did Lila's business. She continued to contribute to her brokerage account on a quarterly basis. Within a few years, she was ready to move some of her money into the medium-risk category. Her portfolio was now worth $10,000.

I advised her to keep $5,000 always in low-risk just in case of emergency needs. Because any tax saving would still be beneficial to her and Robert, she invested $2,500 in an intermediate municipal bond mutual fund and $2,500 in a balanced growth and income fund. But Lila liked the stock market. She was now ready to buy stocks for herself. I agreed since we had a solid foundation in place. She would continue to make her regular infusions into the account. I would hold the money in the money market until we reached $3,000. That amount would be a reasonable one to make a stock purchase with and, in the meantime, she would be getting the best interest rate possible for liquid funds.

After ten years of working together, Lila had added enough to her two mutual funds to bring the original principal invested amount to $5,000. She also had a portfolio of one hundred shares of three high-quality stocks which were giving her the double return of dividends and growth. She told me she was now mentally and financially prepared for some higher-risk investments. I agreed.

Growth is the prime objective of this next category. These are the higher-risk investments tools I began to talk to Lila about.

Lower-Rated Bonds

There is a time and a place to consider lower-rated bonds. The B rating, while implying there isn't the same credit quality as an A-rated bond, still doesn't mean the bond is a speculative one. A bond designated by this lower rating will have either a higher coupon rate, it will be selling at a distinct discount from its par, or $1,000 face value, or it will have a long-term due date.

There are two ways to calculate yield on a bond. One is the current yield. The current yield is a percentage return reached by dividing the yearly annual interest received on the bond by the current bond price.

The yield to maturity is the more important yield calculation at the higher-risk level because you can factor some growth into your bond investment. In addition to the annual interest and the price of the bond, the yield to maturity is figured by including the time factor available until maturity. Let's look at a hypothetical bond: Bond ABC with a coupon of $7\frac{1}{2}$ percent selling at $80 maturity in the year 2009. The $80 translated into bond language means each bond worth $1,000 at maturity is today trading at $800.

Divide $75, the annual interest paid by each bond, by $800, the price of the bond. The current yield is 9.375 percent.

There are bond tables used to determine yield to maturity. Your stockbroker will be able to give you the yield to maturity immediately from her computer. If you own a financial calculator or have access to an online service, you can probably retrieve it for yourself. What is more relevant here is to show the growth which can also be realized by this type of bond purchase. Besides receiving $75 interest per bond each year, the buyer of this bond will see her principal grow from an initial purchase price of $800 per bond to a maturity value of $1,000.

Lower-rated bonds, or longer-term bonds, are available in both taxable and tax-free forms. Bond mutual funds will also state if they are composed of intermediate- or long-term bonds as opposed to short-term ones.

Another way to look at a bond investment is to use the *laddered* approach. Each step of the ladder can represent a sequential bond purchase. A laddered structure reduces the impact of interest-rate swings on the portfolio's yield and market value. Money is coming due at regular periods and can then be reinvested at the prevailing market rates. By using the ladder, you can put some money in a six-month investment tool and then work your way upward and outward in terms of time, in six-month, one-year, or whatever intervals you and your financial adviser decide work best for you.

Remember that bonds pay you interest semiannually, that is, twice a year. By doing a little more investigatory work, you can select bonds that have different months as their interest-paying ones and thereby create a steady income stream for yourself.

The entire ladder doesn't have to be constructed all at once. Lila already had the bottom rungs spoken for. Her subsequent bond purchases would build on the foundation she had in place. Because she was now willing to take on more risk, she could build a longer ladder.

A final benefit to the bond ladder is that the ladder can be restructured as warranted. If there's a change in your income needs or your financial objectives, the continually maturing proceeds can be reinvested to reflect those needs.

Growth Stocks

Growth stocks are key investment tools in this category. You are not anticipating dividend income from this type of stock. What you are looking for is an increase in stock price over a reasonable amount of time. You are investing to see the asset value of that purchase go up.

How do you know what stock to buy? Whole books are devoted to answering this question. I will offer some suggestions that have worked unfailingly for me over twenty years.

Buy what you know.
Is the company you (or your husband or boyfriend or

partner) work for a public one? Do you like the management? Has the stock price been on an upward pattern, or is there a very good reason why it hasn't and you think it's ready for a turnaround? Is the product a good one? Is it selling? You see what I am getting at? You could know things about your own company (positive or negative) that a stock analyst would have to dig deep to find—and still maybe not find. With all the talk about insider information, be sure whatever instincts you use are legal and acceptable ones, not ones you heard discussed at a closed door executive committee meeting.

Buy what you use.

Do you go to McDonald's or do you always choose Pizzeria Uno? Do you shop at Ann Taylor, the Gap, or Urban Outfitters? Do you own a Mac, an IBM, or a Compaq computer? Are you on America Online or CompuServe and do you use Netscape or SpyGlass to get there? Every name I've mentioned is a public company. If you consistently buy the same brand, maybe you should invest in the company stock as well.

Diversify.

Asset allocation prevents you from having too many eggs in one basket. That's why you own bonds, stock, and T-bills. However, diversification is necessary within the asset class as well. I would rather have you buy two odd lots of fifty shares of stock than put all your investment money into one round lot of one hundred shares. An odd lot is any amount that is *not* one hundred shares

If the money you have allocated to higher-risk stocks is less than $2,500, buy a mutual fund of growth stocks instead so that you can still achieve diversity. Those funds will have growth or capital appreciation either in their names or as their objectives.

Do not be frightened of NASDAQ stocks.

I suggested Apple Computer to Jessica, an elementary school teacher, a few weeks ago. She said fine until she asked where she could find it in the newspaper. When I told her it would be under the NASDAQ listings, she said, "Oh, no, I don't want to buy an over-the-counter stock."

The myth that nonlisted stock means speculation lingers. I reminded Jessica that Apple met all our parameters, plus the fact that she used a Macintosh Color Classic all day at school and had bought an Apple Powerbook by choice to use at home.

The NASDAQ market often seems more mysterious to investors because it doesn't have a specific geographic location. Thousands of companies trade on this exchange but there is no floor, like the NYSE and AMEX floor, and there are no floor brokers or specialists. Traders negotiate with each other by phone and through computers. They buy and sell to each other and to the public using a bid-and-ask price arrangement. The bid, or low price, is the price you get when you are selling stock. The ask, or high price, is the price you pay when you are buying stock.

Many new and speculative stocks do trade on the NASDAQ or OTC (over-the-counter) exchange. The name of any exchange alone, however, is not going to give you any guarantee of how much money you can make (or lose) by buying a stock trading there. Money can be made (and lost) on any exchange.

Real Estate

Real estate is the last investment tool I would like to discuss here. Real estate has its risk parameters just as stocks and bonds do. The form of a real estate investment that I believe fits into this category is a type of stock called a REIT, a real estate investment trust.

In many ways a REIT resembles a mutual fund because each REIT is itself a portfolio of real estate properties. Investors buy shares in the fund and the company sponsoring the fund invests the cash into real estate. Once it is formed, the REIT trades on an exchange the same as any other stock.

In order for a REIT to be exempt from corporate income taxation, 90 percent of its income and capital gains must be distributed to its shareholders. The quality REITs provide an annual dividend yield of approximately 5½ to 7½ percent. This high yield makes a REIT stock purchase an income-oriented one. Even though I stated at the beginning of this chapter that higher-risk investments emphasize growth, this type of investment is not a contradiction in terms.

It is difficult to evaluate actual real estate for a number of reasons—lack of track histories, changing valuations of properties, few statistical records, dependency upon the direction of interest rates, etcetera. These reasons alone propel any real estate purchase into a more aggressive category. I am keeping REITs in this category, as opposed to the speculative one, because of 1) the diversification provided within a portfolio of properties, and 2) the dividend protection against a falling stock price.

The same caveat applies to any REIT purchase that applies to a mutual fund purchase. Pay attention to the general manager. Buy only the well-known names. Your broker can provide you information on the individual stock companies. In addition, two major advisers in the real estate industry are Robert A. Stanger and Co. and Audit Investment Research Inc.

To recap *high-risk* investments:
What you get with high-risk investments:

- higher yields
- capital gain (growth) potential
- increase in net worth
- returns from real estate investment as a hedge against inflation (in particular, real estate).

What you give up:

- liquidity
- protection against volatility and price fluctuations
- guaranteed returns.

High-risk investment tools:

- intermediate (seven-to-ten-year) bonds or bond funds (taxable or tax-free)

- lower-rated bonds with higher coupon rates
- long-term certificates of deposit (five years plus)
- growth stocks or growth stock funds
- real estate in the form of a REIT stock or mutual fund purchase.

9

Speculative Investment Tools

LET US FOLLOW LILA'S STORY up to the present. When she came into my office for our annual review last spring, I knew that she had something new in mind for that year's investments.

We went over her portfolio. I made some sell suggestions for stocks that I thought had reached their potential—or were never going to. We balanced the taxable gains on the winners with taking some losses on the nonperforming stocks.

"I'd like to ask your advice about something that's not in my portfolio," she said. "I've had a terrific year in my business and a very interesting situation's come up. I decorated some model apartments for a building which is going condo. Now I've been given the opportunity to buy one of the apartments myself at the inside price."

"You mean you're looking at it as an investment. You're not thinking about living there yourself?" I asked.

"Exactly. But I don't plan to hold it long at all. I think I should be able to flip it right away. I'll make some fast money and then put it all into my investment portfolio."

Lila had fallen right into the trap set by speculative investments. There is *never* the certainty of getting out fast along with a quick profit.

What was true about her remarks, however, was that Lila

could afford a speculative investment. She was a good candidate to make a risk investment at this time, and she was approaching her high-risk investment properly—in other words, she was not disturbing any of the investment plan already in place. She intended to do her risk investing with *new* money. I would just have to explain more of the time element variables and uncertainties to her.

The fourth category of investment tools to explore is the speculation category. There is nothing immoral about speculation. It does not have to be a wager like the kind you would make in a casino. It can be just as much fun (if approached properly) and potentially more profitable. The one warning is the same one I have cautioned about earlier—you must have both the emotional stomach as well as the financial capabilities to invest with any of these tools.

Successful speculation calls for strict attention to timing, combined with the patience to wait out the time period necessary for your purchase to pan out, and the willingness to cut losses when necessary.

I once had a lawyer ask me, "If I give you twenty-five thousand dollars, can you make me money in six months?" He couldn't have asked me a more ridiculous market question.

It's one thing to realize a stock isn't going to rise to its anticipated price after a period of time. It's another to set a fixed time period ahead of making the investment. The stock market itself is subject to too many outside influences to put a short cap on your investing time. Though your first impression might be that only a high-risk investment could yield a good return during a six-month period, actually the only investment that I could *guarantee* would make you money in six months is the no-risk category. You could be assured of making money in a money market account, a six-month Treasury bill, or a six-month certificate of deposit.

If the lawyer had asked me instead if I could make him

money over a two-year period, yes I could. Although I could not guarantee him a certain return, I would have many more tools, including risk ones, available to me to use.

Speculation means buying or selling with the awareness of the high risk involved but with the expectation of above-average gain or profit. Investment vehicles in this area include stock market products, commodities, real estate, metals and other tangibles such as art or antiques.

Stocks which have no tested track record yet, those referred to as *emerging growth*, are the type of stocks which belong in this category. These could be biotech companies, medical, wireless communications, and so forth. Their return cannot be predicted by past performance, but they are bought because of what is anticipated about their products in the future.

Emerging-country stocks are another variety for speculation. Many countries have their own funds traded on the New York Stock Exchange, such as the China Fund, the Chile Fund, the Korea Fund, the Italy Fund. A country fund is clearly less risky than buying one particular stock. A mutual fund made up of Latin American stocks, high-tech stocks, Pacific Rim stocks, or even global bonds would still be the best way to both diversify and distribute the risk.

High-yield bonds, also called junk bonds in their heyday in the eighties, and *deep discount bonds* fall into the speculation field. Junk bonds are corporate bonds identified by low-quality ratings and, thus, higher-than-average interest rates. The bonds are selling at a deep discount because the company issuing them is in financial trouble—but not necessarily facing bankruptcy.

Again, there are mutual funds, which are composed only of high-yield bonds.

Initial public offerings (IPOs) have great appeal in today's media. Since this is the first public trading of the company stock, outside of the prospectus describing the company, what it plans to do with the raised proceeds, and some financials from its private past, an IPO is considered an untested company. You would have to buy this kind of stock individually and not through a mutual fund purchase.

Stocks selling at less than $2 a share are called *penny stocks*. Unless a stock is selling at this price because of a precipitous drop from a more lofty level, you would most likely only find these stock quotes in the pink sheets—the pink-colored pages of quotes of small, over-the-counter companies and the firms which are willing to trade the shares of these companies. As with high-yield bonds, or IPOs, you would want to seek out some background information about the company's product or management to verify that there is some profit potential. I must inject a personal caveat here: in all my experience, cheaper is not better. I prefer to buy fewer shares of a higher-priced company than more shares of a penny stock.

Buying on *margin* is another way to leverage your account. There are two basic types of brokerage accounts: cash and margin. A cash account is the most common. In a *cash account,* when you make an investment purchase, you pay the full amount due within three business days. Day one is the trade date. Day three is the settlement date. No interest charges are levied against your account.

In a *margin account,* you only pay a percentage of the full price. The brokerage firm is in effect loaning you the difference in the amounts, and for the period of the loan you pay interest to the firm against the amount of the debt. Both the brokerage firm and the Federal Reserve Board determine financial requirements for the equity in the account. It often happens that the NYSE may set a minimum that the brokerage firm doesn't think is enough and it will up its own internal minimums.

If the worth of your investments falls below these minimums, I, as your broker, am going to have to call you to ante up more money. If you are speculating, the odds of your getting a margin call increase. And, if you don't have the cash or other securities available to add to your account, you will have to sell stocks or bonds to meet the margin call.

Buying on margin does give you two benefits: 1) by borrowing against your equity, you create more buying power (leverage) for yourself, and 2) margin interest is deductible on your tax return assuming that you itemize your deductions.

Another leveraged way to "play the market" is to buy *options*. Options are risky, but they are not always highly speculative. Your risk is measurable—as opposed to buying on margin when you can often be called for more money to cover a margin call.

The time factor provides the risk element in option buying. Options have an expiration date. They are a wasting asset; that is, they diminish in value the closer they get to that date. You can lose all your money, but you will not lose more money than you invested in the first place.

Owning an option gives you the right to buy or sell a particular stock at a predetermined price by a certain date. Traders in fact rarely convert the option into the underlying stock. Since the options themselves move up and down in a direct relation to the underlying stock's price, the leverage is gained by simply trading the option unit itself.

There are two types of options: puts and calls. You buy a *put* when you think the stock is going down, and you would buy a *call* when you are willing to bet the stock is going up. You are making a wager that the underlying stock is going to go up or down within a relatively short period of time.

In addition to buying puts or calls on specific stocks, you can now also bet on the direction of the market itself by buying or selling index futures and options. For instance, if you really are bearish and are convinced the market is going to drop significantly in the immediate term, you could buy a put on a Standard & Poor's 500 index.

Agile traders will be in and out of an option trade often within days if not within hours. If you've got your ears glued to CNBC or CNN, options are the appropriate risk tool to utilize if you want to act on just-released good or terrible news on a company. If the stock doesn't react the way you judged it would, you're best closing your bet and taking a small loss rather than waiting until expiration when your option will be worthless anyway.

Commodities are another high-risk investment that require a willingness to cut losses on the spot. In Wall Street jargon, "long-term" to a commodities trader is minutes.

A commodity contract, or futures contract, represents a commitment to buy or sell a commodity at a preset price before this contract expires. If you go long, or buy the contract, you will make money if the price rises above what you paid for the contract. If you're selling, or going short, your profit is made by the contract declining in price.

Options must be purchased in a cash account and paid for in full. Commodities are purchased in a margin account and require only a small down payment. The risk is heightened over options because you stand to lose more than your purchase price, you could face an immediate margin call, and if you don't have the funds available, your contract will be liquidated and you'll lose everything!

Commodity trading is only for the most aggressive trader even if you should choose to participate by buying into a managed commodity fund. This type of fund, unlike the kind of mutual funds we will be talking about in much more detail in a subsequent chapter, also has the potential of also going belly up.

Lila's proposed condo purchase belongs in this category because there is no income stream as in the REITs, there is no guaranteed buyer, and she'll be responsible for the carrying charges until she either sells the apartment or decides to rent it in the interim. I call this type of investment *venture real estate*.

Lila's own knowledge of the building, other inside proposed apartment sales, and the famous "location, location, location" real estate maxim may indeed make this a terrific and timely opportunity. If she is not able to flip it as she hopes she can, however, she needs to be more than mindful of all of the risks and responsibilities involved in real estate ownership.

Investment in *gold* is usually perceived as an inflation hedge.

Gold may not be absolutely glittering these days, but neither is it tarnished. Interest in gold periodically perks up not so much because inflation is feared as much as it used to be but because investors are always seeking an alternate investment to stocks and bonds.

Gold, silver, platinum, and the other *metals* are popular in times of rising inflation. They often have tangible value when the purchasing power of the dollar declines. Hard assets, as opposed to financial ones, are regarded as havens in troubled economic times.

Gold has a special benefit besides its intrinsic value, and that is its worldwide acceptance. The metal is traded from New York to Hong Kong and is retained as a vital asset by every major government.

Fundamental supply-and-demand pressures work to the advantage of mining stocks. The gold jewelry demand, especially from China and other Far East countries, has escalated while production has declined.

It would not be unreasonable to designate about 5 percent of your portfolio to this type of asset, but do that investing by means of a fund. Gold itself pays no dividends. It also can be difficult to sell at competitive prices at certain times. Purchasing shares in a mutual fund is the most sensible way to participate in this market. If South African gold shares still rub you the wrong way, there are other domestic or Canadian precious metals funds.

Hard assets, *tangibles,* can be further broken down into *collectibles* such as art, jewelry, antiques, stamps, coins, and so on. I heard an interesting story recently about a tangible I would not have thought about—a musical instrument.

I was talking to a woman in fund-raising about this book and she told me that her husband's cello, which was purchased for $150,000 about ten years ago, is now insured for $1 million. She said she and her husband often talk about selling the instrument and upgrading their lifestyle with the proceeds. On the other hand, because he is a musician and earns his livelihood that way, they'd have to buy another cello. By the time the new one is reinsured and they've paid capital gains, they may not truly be ahead at all.

Collectibles, as a rule, are going to react to inflationary expectations, tax rates, peace or war, and consumer sentiment—confident or anxious—just the way gold and real estate do. An antique instrument like the one described above may be an exception in that it is steadily increasing in value, but it is not currently a trading vehicle. It is a permanent member of their family.

As I hope I have made abundantly clear, speculative trading is not for the faint-hearted. If you are risk-averse, ignore this category no matter how large your investment pie slice might be. On the other hand, if the thrill of the reward tips the scales for you and you can afford to take losses if necessary, isolate your high-risk money within your portfolio and try one of the investment tools described in this chapter.

To recap *speculative* investments:
Speculative investment tools:

- emerging growth stocks or funds
- emerging-country or global funds
- high-yield ("junk") or deep discount bonds
- initial public offerings
- penny stocks
- options: puts and calls
- commodities
- venture real estate
- precious metals
- collectibles.

What you get:

- high gain or profit reward
- high risk of loss
- rapid market action
- short-term gains.

What you give up:

- credit quality
- liquidity (depending upon the investment tool)
- safety of principal
- predictable rate of return.

10

Working With a Stockbroker

Now you know what your investment money is. You also know how it is calculated, and how much risk you are willing to tolerate. You have learned what investment tools are available to help you reach your financial goals. It's time to talk about where you go to put this newfound knowledge to work.

It probably seems as if every time you turn on the television, open a newspaper, or read a magazine, you're being convinced about the merits of one financial institution over another. Why, you must wonder, would I use a bank instead of a mutual fund company when the bank has its own mutual funds? Why would I pay retail when I can buy wholesale in terms of my commission dollar?

Let's look into each one of these financial shops in detail and get you the answers to all your questions.

Full Service or Discount?

A stockbroker is the person most women go to to help them put their plan in action. There are some steps you can take by yourself which I mentioned earlier, such as buying Treasuries directly from the Federal Reserve, setting up a money market account at your bank, or buying a certificate of deposit from your bank. For virtually every other transaction, however, you will need an intermediary—one of the people or entities we will be discussing in this chapter.

A stockbroker deals in the purchase and sales of a range of investments. A broker does not work independently the way a personal financial planner can. A stockbroker must take an examination to be registered and the firm she works for must hold memberships on the various exchanges and report to all the required regulatory parties. (I am going to use the pronoun "she" to refer to all stockbrokers, although the exams are the same for both sexes, the questions a broker will ask you in the initial interview are not gender specific, and there *are* male brokers who will also be willing to give you the time and attention you need!)

Stock market transactions, by law, require the help of a broker, and the broker is compensated only by commission. The broker legally receives no other fees.

Being a broker myself, I'd like to tell you it is easy to find a good stockbroker. Unfortunately, that isn't the case. There are thousands of brokers *qualified* to work with you, but finding a broker suited to your own style of investing isn't always that simple. We are not all at our most sane when we are discussing our own money. The market's volatility can ruffle the feathers of the most patient clients and brokers. Personalities can intrude and wreak temporary havoc.

Such is the life of all relationships. It is important to remember that you are embarking upon a *relationship* with a broker. You and your broker will work together most effectively if you both are presuming that the relationship will be a long-term one. There are no contracts signed in the brokerage business, however, and if things are not working out, either one of you can "fire" the other!

Take the time necessary to find the right broker for yourself. You wouldn't call an 800 number for a doctor or lawyer. Don't treat your money in any more cavalier fashion than you would your health. You can literally afford to investigate before you sign on because brokers, as opposed to some other professionals, do not charge for an interview session.

Do not just walk into a local brokerage office and ask for any broker either. You will be assigned the "broker of the day," and that usually means a rookie by definition. Not that I had not been a rookie in my day either, but I am writing this book to increase your odds of building wealth.

My new clients today are all referrals from existing clients. Do the same yourself. Ask any professionals in your life, such as your lawyer or accountant, for names. Ask your friends and relatives if you know they are active in investing and are pleased with their financial person. Ask friends or people at work. Make a list of prospects to interview either by phone or in person.

You will want to know how long your contacts have worked with their brokers and how well the broker's investment recommendations have performed. Depending upon how active and involved you want to be with your investments, you will want to ask, too, whether the broker is content to respond to customer requests and take the order or if she prefers to manage her accounts in a more independent way.

A woman who was referred to me by a professional women's club called earlier this year. She had joined an investment club and was ready to start making her own purchases. In the course of the conversation it turned out that she only wanted to buy on her own what the group as a whole had decided to buy for itself. I told her up front that that was not my style. I like to do my own research and pick my own stocks. I do not expect every client to agree every time I call with a recommendation, but I would be unhappy if she were to call and copycat her club's orders with me.

These differences are not a matter of right or wrong. They are a matter of style. I gave her the name of another broker in my office who operated more to this woman's liking.

If you have done the homework described earlier in the book, it is not mandatory to have a continually hands-on attitude toward your own investments. That is what a stockbroker does. I am supposed to monitor your portfolio on a regular basis, make sure your dividends and interest are swept into a money market account or be paid out to you, and call you before your bonds mature. I assume you have a life and want to get on with it. The investing part of your life becomes my responsibility. That is what I am good at and that is my job. You should spend your time doing what you are good at.

When you contact a broker, be prepared to ask a lot of questions—as well as answer a few yourself. It is perfectly legitimate to ask about the broker's background, how long she has been in the business, and what firms she has worked for. You may want to ask, as well, if the broker has a specialty or if she avoids certain products. For instance, I have passed an exam and am registered to deal in commodities, but I don't choose to. None of this information will be on diplomas hanging on a broker's wall.

You and your broker will want to define the amount of communication or education you want or even need. Marcia, a retired English teacher, likes me to send her every mention of any one of her stocks I come across in all of my financial reading. She studies every insert that comes with her monthly statement and often calls to request the marketing brochure mentioned.

Denise is in her late thirties, single, and a head buyer for Neiman-Marcus. She complains about the annual reports and proxy statements that must be sent to her. She tells me she groans every time she sees an envelope with my firm's name on as the return address and slings it over to a disgracefully large pile in her kitchen. Again, a question of style.

A good broker will want to know something about your finances as well as your investment objectives. Don't be put off if you're asked how much money you plan on investing. The broker is not screening you to see if you are a hot ticket or not. She needs to know your whole picture in order to make the appropriate suggestions. If things are going well, and you have your financial profile with you, this is the right time to discuss it together.

The type of stockbroker I am referring to in all these examples works for a *full-service brokerage house*. All of these types of services—from no-charge consultation time to the same individual being responsible for your account to a wealth of free research to a wide range of products, investment tools, and tax information—are all provided by a full-service firm.

A full-service broker is responsible for your account—she will educate you about financial matters and do her best to help you accomplish your financial goals. She will most likely recommend a personal asset review once a year. These reviews are best done in person but, if that is inconvenient, a phone conference can suffice.

The most opportune time to conduct this review is around October or November. If there are losses to be taken to balance gains, or vice versa, you will have time to do this tax preparation before the year-end. The fourth quarter is also a good time to set up a Keogh plan if you qualify, make a deferred compensation or bonus decision if you are offered one, and think about strategies for the new year.

As far as I am concerned, a key reason to deal with a full-service broker is the contact and communication implicit in this relationship. My clients have access to me without paying a fee for my time or the phone call. Just as I call them with buy and sell recommendations, they also talk to me about stock ideas they have or questions about planning.

Because the majority of my clients have worked with me for a long time, I have become involved in aspects of their lives outside of the stock market. Carole called last spring to ask if she should take out a car loan. Cars have nothing to do with her stock portfolio but a car purchase is a financial one and she wanted my thoughts. In my experience, men and women are more than willing to pay retail commissions in return for the security of knowing they aren't talking to an anonymous face and voice who has no first hand knowledge of their financial histories.

None of what I am saying is meant to imply that you must give all your money to one broker. Nor do I mean to reject discount brokerage houses.

It is not cheating to have more than one stockbroker. You can even have more than one full-service broker. You might have inherited your broker from your parents. For any reason, from lack of the attention you want to a desire for independence, you may decide to find another financial person for yourself. It is unlikely you would transfer all your assets in one fell swoop. It makes much more sense to start the new relationship slowly. Then, if it develops to your satisfaction, you can transfer your complete account.

Another reason to have more than one broker is if you are dealing with one broker who has a specialty—tax-free bonds, for example—and you want to conduct your stock business elsewhere. This does not mean you cannot discuss with one broker what you are doing with another. In the above case, it would be best to coordinate information because of the end-of-the-year gain and loss adjustment. Stock gains and losses don't apply only to stocks. Any asset's gain or loss can be used against any other.

What is unbecoming is placing any one broker in the position of discrediting another. If you feel you have had a bad judgment call from your broker, talk about it directly with that broker. Every broker is in competition in a sense with every other broker, but we are all professionals too. Hindsight is a great equalizer.

Discount brokers can execute your trades for you at a wholesale price for one important reason—that is what they do: execute trades. More often than not you will dial an 800 number and give your buy or sell order to a voice on the phone who will repeat it to you for accuracy and then, if you wish, give you the price at which your order was transacted.

A discount broker will not telephone you with a buy, sell, or hold recommendation. You may request some research material these days from the bigger-name firms but, again, you are not speaking to an account executive of your own. You will receive the same confirmation slip recapping your trades that you would from a full-service firm. You'll also get monthly, or quarterly, statements.

If you are very involved with the market, subscribe to market letters, and make *all* your own investment decisions, a discount firm makes sense for you. If you have no need of establishing a rapport with a particular broker and if you do not require feedback regarding your theories—if you are not using the full services—there is no need for you to pay for them.

It is unfair to take one broker's idea and transact the trade someplace else. Use the discount firm when the idea is all yours. If your full-service broker made the recommendation, however, it is only right to buy from her and pay the freight.

I said earlier in the book to buy from the well-known mutual fund companies. I will reiterate this when we come to the chapter on mutual funds, but the same advice goes for dealing with discount brokers. As in any other industry, time in business and track records count. Reputable names of discount brokers include Charles Schwab, Muriel Siebert & Co., Quick & Reilly Inc., and Fidelity Investments.

There is a new crop of discounters, referred to as super-deep discounters. Be wary. There are ongoing investigations into some of these firms. The commissions may be rock bottom but there are allegations that traders have not gotten the best prices for their stocks. It is not worth it to save on the commission but lose on the principal amount. I am not indicting all super-deep discounters, but do be careful. "Beautiful" commissions may only be skin deep.

Cyberspace continues to spawn new ways of conducting stock business. On America Online I could buy and sell stocks at one extremely low minimum fee through a service called *E Trade*. If I were not a broker (every broker is required by law to trade only with her own firm), I myself might be tempted to manage my portfolio through E Trade. But that is because the market is my business. Be very careful, unless you know exactly what you are doing, when choosing this path.

Over and beyond the knowledge factor is the financial security one. Online services themselves have issued cautions about releasing personal credit information on the World Wide

Web. Hackers abound. And if there is a glitch in your computer system, the trade may not even get entered the way you intend it to. As of this writing, I think a paper trail is safer for both your financial and investment protection.

One last word of caution regarding whatever type of firm with which you decide to do business. Find out for how much your account is insured. Your cash in a bank has no insurance coverage over $100,000. Brokerage firms have their own minimum and maximum amounts too. Different types of accounts carry different insurance protection. The insurance covers your account in case the brokerage firm goes bankrupt. It does not cover you against losses in your own personal brokerage account. It is definitely worth it for your peace of mind to know that your securities are safe being held at the brokerage firm in what is referred to as "in street name." You should not need to worry about this in dealing with any of the high-profile, full-service firms.

If you never feel secure unless you can touch your own investments, ask your broker to have them transferred out to you and you can put them in a safe deposit box. Do not ever leave any stock certificate lying around the house in either a file or a drawer. A lost certificate can be replaced but the process is arduous. An even greater worry is a case of theft. Certificates are negotiable.

Once a certificate is delivered to you, it is out of street name and is into your own name. The issuing company, let us use General Electric (GE), now has your name as a shareholder of record. GE will send you your dividends, the quarterly reports, and a proxy for the annual meeting. Your broker will no longer be able to help you with any tracking of the stock or lost dividends, and your position will no longer be reflected on your statement from the brokerage office.

I would suggest that if you trade with a discount firm, you routinely ask that your certificates be registered in your own name and sent to you. I do not mean to imply that a discount firm is not capable of holding your securities in the way a full-service house can. I am suggesting this because there is no one broker responsible for your account. You will not be speaking to the same individual when you call to question something. By requesting delivery of your certificates, you know where they are at all times. If you should decide to sell them at another firm, there is no time lost.

If I were trading electronically, even I would be a bit nervous until I received delivery of my securities.

Firing a Broker

As I have explained, there is no contractual arrangement between a stockbroker and a client. There exists simply a customer agreement in which you agree to pay within three business days for what you buy. The firm, in return, pays you your proceeds of a sale in three business days.

You may walk away from a full-service broker, a discount broker, or an E-mail trader at any time without obligation or explanation. When the person on the other side of the phone or computer is faceless, explanations aren't expected.

If you decide to part ways with your full-service broker for whatever reason, it seems only fair to alert your broker. If there is a problem in the relationship, she is going to be as aware of it as you. She may even have suggested to you that you would be better suited with someone else in her office, and she will make the introduction for you. If you are moving your account because you are moving to another part of the country, you are marrying a stockbroker, or your daughter is becoming a broker—these reasons are all readily understandable and your broker will help you make the transition as efficiently as possible.

If you cannot handle talking to your broker again, you do not absolutely have to, even in the case of a full-service brokerage firm. The way the brokerage business works, the firm receiving the account does all the paperwork. The firm losing the account does nothing except deliver the positions in the account, through a wire transfer, to the new firm.

Working with a discount broker makes the firing even more simple and painless. Since you do not have one particular person representing you, you just don't make the next phone call.

What you get from a *discount broker:*

• Treasuries
• retirement plans
• stocks, bonds, options, commodities, etc.
• some mutual funds.

What you get from a *full-service brokerage house:*

All of the above plus:

• a specific stockbroker responsible for your account
• full range of financial advice
• unlimited check writing on a money market account
• insurance products
• wider range of retirement plans and tools with which to fund those plans
• credit, debit, and/or ATM card
• tangibles only in the form of mutual funds or gold coins.

11

Working With a Bank

THE CHATTY NEIGHBORHOOD BANK around the corner is about as obsolete as the Mom-and-Pop store where the Wal-Mart exists today. You're much more likely to encounter a friendly ATM machine than a teller who doesn't demand two forms of identification to cash your check at the bank where your own account is held.

Banks today are large, sophisticated financial institutions. They are competing not only with each other but with mutual fund managers and brokerage firms. They are merging, crossing state lines, and issuing their own debit cards.

What specifically can you get from a bank besides the traditional checking and savings accounts?

You can get most of the low-risk investment tools directly through your bank account or as an adjunct to your account. If you maintain a large enough balance, for instance, you may be entitled to a money market account with interest rates comparable to those of the money market mutual funds. You certainly should have an interest-bearing checking account, even if the rate is at minimal levels.

Many banks issue their own MasterCard or Visa credit cards which allow you to make purchases and have the purchase amount automatically deducted from your account without your having to receive a monthly bill. All charges will be reflected on your monthly bank statement.

Several different types of retirement plans can be set up at a bank, but the investments within the plan will have to be limited to bank products, such as longer term certificates of deposit and some mutual funds. And, as I've mentioned before, you can purchase a Treasury bill, note, or bond at your bank for approximately the same service charge that you would pay at a brokerage firm.

The one cash investment that can only be made at a bank is the purchase of *series EE bonds*. These are U.S. Government bonds, also referred to as savings bonds, which offer relatively high interest rates and provide some tax advantages.

EE bonds are purchased at a discount from the face amount and have a minimum guaranteed interest rate. What makes them a good purchase for some women is that the minimum purchase amounts are quite low—lower than a zero coupon bond. The face values range from $50 to $10,000 while a zero coupon bond is only sold in increments of $1,000 face value. Again, like the zero coupon bonds, the interest is exempt from state and local income taxes—and it may be exempt at the federal level as well if you use the bonds for tuition purposes. The specific restrictions are quite intricate so be sure to investigate thoroughly before you assume you qualify.

The bonds cannot be redeemed for the first six months. After that period of time, they are liquid, but you do not get your interest on any six-month period unless you hold it to the end of the period. Because of this form of illiquidity and because the interest on the EE bonds was just lowered as of this writing, I would not recommend purchasing them unless their small face value makes them the only investment you can afford.

Why, you might be wondering, should I continue to maintain a bank account now that I have enough equity in my brokerage account to transform it into a check-writing account? I have two answers to that, notwithstanding my own firm's (and every other firm's which services this type of account) contention that it can serve as the complete custodian for all your money.

I am financially brokerage conservative enough that I do not like to put all my eggs in one basket—no matter how large the basket and how many eggs it can safely hold. I have a check-writing brokerage account and I use that account to pay my major bills, such as quarterly estimates, insurance premiums, and real estate taxes during the year. I also have an interest-bearing checking account at a Boston bank. I want to keep a banking relationship. I am more comfortable paying all my monthly bills out of my bank account and not filtering all my financials through my brokerage account. Call it a different form of asset allocation.

On the other hand, I also would not consider buying a brokerage product from a bank. A mutual fund managed by a bank, its trust department, or its advisory services does not interest me. Buy a mutual fund from an organization that is in the fund business and has a record to prove it.

There is plenty of room in the financial universe for both banks and brokerage firms. I think both are needed. Without a lot of effort on your part, you can utilize both to complement your own financial well-being.

What you get from a *bank:*

- passbook, savings, and checking accounts
- money market deposit accounts
- series EE bonds
- certificates of deposit
- Treasuries
- retirement plans
- debit card and ATM card
- loans
- some financial advice and sometimes mutual funds managed by that bank.

12

Working With Mutual Funds

THE TERM "MUTUAL FUND" has become part of everyday parlance. It is almost un-cool not to own a mutual fund or at least to have a darn good reason why you don't. Thanks to Peter Lynch, Fidelity's Magellan Fund is a virtual symbol of the industry.

Are you missing the boat if you are not a Magellan investor? Is a mutual fund something every woman should own? There is no short answer to this question. Just because something becomes a buzzword does not qualify it as a mandatory investment tool. Let us look into mutual funds in depth. At the end of this chapter you'll know much better if and when you should own this financial instrument yourself.

Mutual funds (open-end funds), unit investment trusts, and *Closed-end funds* all fall under the broader heading of *regulated investment companies.* A regulated investment company is a firm that receives funds from many investors with similar objectives, pools these assets, and uses them to purchase investments chosen by that firm's professional investment managers. When you purchase shares in the investment company, you own a share of its portfolio of investments.

The most common regulated investment companies are referred to as mutual funds. You will see the other terms from time to time, so let me give a brief description of them.

A *closed-end fund* has a set capital structure with a specified number of shares. When you buy shares in this type of fund, you are buying shares another investor in the same fund is selling. There is a finite number of shares rather than the infinite number in open-end funds. If you want to liquidate your position, you will have to find another investor willing to buy it.

You do not have to do this search individually. Shares of closed-end funds are traded on the stock exchanges just like any other publicly traded company. Because you have to trade these shares on the open market, the price per share doesn't have to equal the net asset value (NAV) of the share. (The price per share of an open-end fund is its net asset value.) Again, for this reason, the more sophisticated and risk-oriented investor will seek out closed-end funds selling at a discount from their NAV in the hope of realizing a greater return.

A *unit investment trust* is a variation of a closed-end fund. Unit trusts traditionally have invested in a fixed portfolio of bonds, taxable or tax-free, which are held until maturity. A bond mutual fund, in contrast, has no set life period and the bonds are constantly being traded in the hope of greater gain or higher interest return. Because the bonds are not being actively managed once the portfolio is set, the annual fees charged for unit trusts are usually lower than those charged by mutual funds.

Cash flow is relatively predictable and your interest is paid out to you at regular intervals—either monthly or quarterly. Your principal is also paid out when a bond matures or if it is called prematurely. I like to refer to unit trusts as declining assets because when the trust is over, there is no money left. You've been receiving it over its lifetime.

Open-end funds, which I will in the future refer to as mutual funds, do not have a set number of shares. The number of outstanding shares varies as investors purchase or redeem them directly from the issuing company. The value of a share in a mutual fund is determined by the net asset value. NAV is computed by dividing the value of the fund's total net assets by the number of shares outstanding.

Mutual funds provide numerous benefits:

1. Professional management: Full-time professionals supervise all quality mutual funds at a relatively low cost.
2. Diversification: Virtually every type of financial vehicle can make up a mutual fund. Diversification always provides a hedge against uncertainty.
3. Flexibility: Most funds are part of what is called a family of funds. For no fee, or a low one, you can switch between funds in the family by one phone call to your stockbroker or to the fund (at will).
4. Professional evaluation: There are several annual surveys conducted of mutual funds (notably by *Business Week* and *Forbes*) as well as rating services. The most popular service around is Morningstar. Morningstar's reports are readily available and the service provides a huge compendium of mutual fund data, updated every other week, on more than 1,300 funds.
5. Low minimum investment: The minimum can be as little as $250 for an IRA and $500 to $1000 for an individual purchase.

When you buy a stock, the sales charge for this transaction is called a commission. Mutual fund investors may or may not be subject to a sales charge depending upon what kind of fund they are buying. This charge, when you are referring to mutual funds, is called a *load*.

Mutual funds are classified in one of three ways depending upon whether there is a load or not and when and how it is charged.

1. *No-Load Fund*—No-load funds carry a zero sales charge to investors. Purchases and sales of shares in these funds are made at the fund's NAV. Every dollar you invest is allocated to the fund for investment and not kept in a sort of escrow to cover sales charges. There may be a very small management fee charged annually against the fund. This fee reduces the performance of the fund but is not a sales charge. Brokerage firms usually do not deal in no-load funds. They have to be bought directly from the fund manager.

2. *12b-1 Fund*—This type of fund is sort of a hybrid fund between load and no-load. It is not nearly as common as the other two. At your initial point of purchase every dollar is committed to investment. There is an annual fee, however, assessed to cover the fund's sales and marketing costs. The fees are not large (typically 0.1 to 1 percent of the total assets of the fund), but since this fee is assessed every year, oddly enough, the longer you hold your fund shares, the more you will have paid. Check your fund's performance to make sure you are willing to keep paying for the privilege of ownership.

3. *Load Fund: Front-End and Back-End*—Shareholders pay a stated sales charge at the time of purchase in a *front-end fund*. The load may range from as little as 3.5 percent to as much as 8.5 percent of your purchase amount. The load charge is stipulated in the fund's prospectus and it is a one-time charge. There should be no other charges during the lifetime of your ownership.

A *back-end charge* is exactly that—you pay at redemption time as opposed to purchase time. There is a point here that is important, however. This load usually declines by a percentage point or so each year up to approximately six years. Since a mutual fund investment should not be regarded as a near term one, you might find that by the time you choose to switch funds, you will have bypassed the back-end charge time constraints.

Fund Literature

I spoke of a prospectus above. The prospectus is the Bible of fund information. It will give you the fund's investment objectives, policies, and sometimes even what time period it anticipates is needed to achieve its goal. Pay special attention to these details.

For example, Fidelity Blue Chip, according to Morningstar, has grown at a 24 percent annual rate over the past five years. It is designed for you if you have a ten-year time frame. If you have a young child, you could use this fund as a vehicle to prepare for college tuition.

In contrast, to use a less risky fund, Fidelity's Puritan has grown 15.6 percent over the same time period. Its time outlook is for five years or more.

If a fund prospectus tells you the fund plans to use some hedging techniques—an aggressive investment posture—and you are a conservative investor, you have no business participating in this fund. Nor do you have any defense against poor performance or complaints about your money being at risk if you made the decision yourself to buy this fund and you bought it directly.

After many years of excesses and lawsuits, the Securities and Exchange Commission (SEC) has standardized the content and format of mutual fund prospectuses. In addition to stating its investment objectives, the fund will also include a fee table, the fund's return—net of expenses—net income over a specific time period, and the NAV changes over this same time. It would be impossible to know any fund's holdings on any one day, but the funds issue quarterly documents which list their positions at the end of the quarter. When you hear the financial reporters referring to "portfolio window dressing," this is exactly what they are talking about. The fund managers want their portfolios to look as profitable and fancy as possible at the end of each calendar quarter.

Brokerage Mutual Funds versus Fund Companies

Should you buy a fund managed and run by your stockbroker's firm or should you do some research yourself and buy directly from Fidelity, Evergreen, Twentieth Century, etcetera? This is a very "loaded" question.

First off, as I said earlier, a brokerage firm generally is going to charge you a load. Some outside funds do and some don't, and some charge for certain of their funds and not for others. In fact, some previously no-load funds now carry loads so that the brokerage firms can deal in them as well when previously stockbrokers couldn't buy them for their clients.

I don't have a strong bias for load versus no-load versus back-load. What matters foremost is the portfolio manager and the fund's track record. You definitely want to know the portfolio manager's name, tenure, and credentials. The record of any particular fund is easy to track once you have a prospectus in hand. Simply compare the NAV from year to year.

As an overview, I'd look for good, steady returns. Rapid bursts of short-lived gains should be a warning signal. Look for evidence of resiliency in more difficult economic times. Above all, your own objectives, time horizon, and risk-tolerance should be in sync with those of the fund you select.

Therein lies one of the problems. Many funds are relatively new—especially the brokerage-firm funds. If I am making, or recommending, a longer-term investment, I want to have confidence that my money or yours is going to have the best chance of increasing in both good, bad, and in-between economic cycles.

The only exception is if you are making a risk investment. Obviously if you are venturing into uncharted territory, for instance a fund made up of third world countries, you would not expect a track record. This brings us full circle once more to the importance of the reputation of the fund manager.

There is one last bit of information that is important to know—information that you will not see in print anyplace. The downside to buying a brokerage firm mutual fund is that if you decide to leave your broker and take your account to another brokerage firm, your fund will not be able to transfer over intact. The same happens if your broker herself leaves for another firm. All types of securities except the mutual funds of any one brokerage firm, called proprietary funds, are transferable. On the other hand, your fund may have given you the return you have expected and you are perfectly content to liquidate it and invest elsewhere.

Mutual funds pay capital gains, dividends, and interest the same as individual stocks and bonds do. A capital gain is the difference (the profit) between the purchase price and the sale price. The income received on a stock is referred to as dividend income. The income from a bond or a certificate of deposit is called interest income. You are customarily given one of three choices when you purchase a mutual fund:

1. reinvest all capital gains and dividends
2. reinvest all gains and pay out dividends
3. pay out all gains and dividends.

There truly is no reason not to take option one, unless you need the gains and dividends for your living expenses cash flow and are looking more for constancy of principal. Reinvestment in any mutual fund is done without load charge. Automatic reinvestment is the best and least expensive way to let your funds to work for you.

I mentioned Morningstar under the professional evaluation benefits of mutual funds. Morningstar today is to mutual funds what Standard & Poor's is to stocks and bonds. Your broker will be able to provide you with a Morningstar opinion on any fund. If you are computer oriented and are signed on to an online service, you can probably retrieve the same yourself.

Value Line, in addition to its stock research, offers a mutual fund survey which follows about 1,500 established funds and 500 newer ones. It is updated three times per year. Standard & Poor's/Lipper Mutual Fund Profiles provides data on approximately 750 funds and is updated quarterly.

How to Choose a Mutual Fund

Mutual funds are classified according to their investment objectives, goals, financial tools used, and risk level. If you decide to work with mutual funds, I can assure you it is much easier to find the right mutual fund than to find the right roommate, hairdresser, or cleaning service. There is a fund for every season and for every style. The following categories will prove this to you.

Money Funds

Taxable

Money funds are money market funds, your low-risk investment tool. Money funds are sold by banks, brokerage firms, and even by mutual funds. I say low-risk, rather than no-risk, because even those funds sold by banks whose depositors are covered by $100,000 FDIC (Federal Deposit Insurance Corp.) still cannot absolutely guarantee shareholders against loss. On the other hand, if a fund ever suffered a price decline below the $1 per share price, the depositors would flee immediately. Most taxable money market funds are going to pay you the same yield within a few basis points with only a few cents differentiating them. If you see a money market fund promoting itself with an unusually high yield, beware. That fund is not investing in short-term money market instruments, such as certificates of deposit or T-bills, but is extending its maturities and using hedging and risk vehicles to provide that yield.

A money market fund is used for liquidity and for what I call "money on the back burner," money waiting to be spent elsewhere or money that you keep separately for emergencies. Spending your energy looking for the highest yield is not only a waste of time but might also be putting your principal at risk.

Unless you are in between investments at a mutual fund company, there is no reason not to use the money market fund of either your bank or your brokerage firm.

Tax-Free or Tax-Advantaged

There are money market funds which are tax-free and others which invest only in government securities. Another waste of your investment time is looking for a totally exempt tax-free fund. That means a fund which invests only in bonds of the state in which you live. These funds are rare and the yield, bottom line, is not worth the effort.

If you are in the top tax bracket, and depending upon the interest rate climate at the time, a national tax exempt fund might be worthwhile. You would be liable for taxes at the state and local level but federally exempt. I would only suggest this move if interest rates are at the high end. At lower rate times, the juggling of funds just is not worth the effort.

If you are *ultra*-conservative, and willing to lose a point or less in yield, you can invest in a government money market fund. All the paper will be issues of the U.S. government and some of the interest will be exempt at the state level.

All the major brokerage firms and mutual fund companies will have these varieties of tax advantaged money funds available to their clients.

Domestic Stock Funds

There are many different kinds of stock mutual funds ranging from those that aim for a low-risk stance to a middle-ground approach to those that take greater risks in the hope of producing a higher return.

Growth Funds

Growth funds seek long-term capital appreciation by investing in mid-size to large-size companies whose stocks are perceived either to be undervalued or are expected to show consistently strong earnings growth. The objective of a growth fund is to achieve an increase in the value of its investments rather than to pay out dividends.

Growth and Income Funds

These funds are also called equity-income funds or total return funds. Growth and income funds invest for growth but have a secondary, but equal, objective of providing investors with dividend income. The dividends, especially if reinvested into the fund, help both total fund return and act as a cushion in poor market times.

Balanced Funds

This fund is only a half step below the above fund in terms of risk. In addition to paying high current income and seeking long-term growth, a balanced fund will also try to conserve its investors' initial principal. A balanced fund, even though in the stock category, will also invest in bonds. The mixture of stocks and bonds will temper the volatility even more than the growth/income funds in unsettled markets. Some of these funds trade their portfolios heavily—moving rapidly from stocks to bonds to cash—so it is worth reviewing the research reports to be sure whatever sense of stability you require is being matched by this fund.

Aggressive Growth Funds

As the name suggests, these funds are characterized by high risk and high return. Capital gains are the objective. Dividends and interest are not. A mutual fund is one of the best ways to participate aggressively in this arena because of the diversification benefit. If one company in the portfolio mix goes belly up, you haven't lost all your money.

Global Stock Funds

A mutual fund investment is definitely the preferred way to invest internationally. In fact, as an individual you may often not even be able to buy the stocks that a fund can, because the shares are not traded on one of the U.S. stock exchanges.

Global funds or world funds invest anywhere in the world, *including* the United States.

International or *foreign funds* invest anywhere in the world *except* the United States.

Regional funds invest in specific geographic areas, such as Europe or the Far East.

Country funds invest entirely in the country for which they are named, e.g. the China Fund, the Italy Fund, the New Germany Fund. These particular funds are usually closed-end mutual funds and trade on either the NYSE or the AMEX. It is important to check how much above or below these funds are trading from their net asset value.

The regional and the country funds are higher-risk investments than the global or international funds. In all of these funds, currency and political considerations, as much as the local economy, will affect overall fund performance.

Bond Mutual Funds

Taxable Bond Funds

The big differences among all bond funds are interest rates, the time frame of the fund, and the quality of the investment. In the simplest scenario, if you think interest rates are headed up, stay with a short-term bond fund. If you think they are falling lower, buy a fund that invests in intermediate- or longer-term bonds.

Municipal Bond Funds

Tax-free bond funds exist both in the national and single-state variety. The same caveat exists here as for the tax-free money market funds. Often the single state fund will not, in the final analysis, deliver a better return to you than the national fund. Do the math. Be sure of your income tax bracket and check the expenses the fund may incur.

Junk Bond Fund

Today, brokerage firms like to call these bonds *high-yield bonds* to dispel the negative associations with the eighties and its miscreant financiers. The junk bond funds don't seem to care what's in a name, and many of the bonds date from the eighties, so why hide it!

An investment-grade bond carries a rating of BB + or better by Standard & Poor's and Ba1 or better by Moody's. In the strictest sense, any bond rated less than this is a "junk" bond. Again, there is a range of risks even in this risk category.

Some portfolio managers stick to corporates maturing in seven to ten years. Others will seek out lower-rated debt, betting against default. One specific fund, Fidelity Capital and Income, will even buy bonds that have already defaulted in the event there may be a turnaround.

Global Bond Funds

Interest rates do not move in tandem all over the world. A European benchmark seems to be what the German Bundesbank is going to do. As interest rates ebb and flow in Germany, so do many on the continent. But that may not be true in Asia, in Mexico, or in the United States. For the investor seeking a higher-dividend return as well as international exposure, a global bond fund is a good choice.

Fluctuating interest rates as well as currency values influence portfolio performance. When overseas interest rates are higher than our domestic ones, global bond funds are quite attractive. When the foreign currency weakens, however, and loses value relative to our dollar, so does the value of the portfolio. Global bond funds will state clearly if they invest in long-term or short-term maturities. Pay heed to this, keeping your own risk-tolerance in mind.

High-Risk Funds

Sector Funds

A *sector fund* invests in one particular industry. Some of the sector funds are more universal in nature, such as a retail fund or a manufacturing fund. Others are extremely fine-tuned and mirror the latest fad in the investment world. Biotech, medical, and communications have been popular areas. Since most of the really hot new areas are made up of brand new companies, I'd certainly prefer the broad mutual fund approach rather than trying to guess at the one company that is going to make it.

Emerging Market Funds

These funds have been in a real slump for a few years, but these lows create the perfect buying opportunity for some investors with strong stomachs. Forget about looking for individual stocks. Buy a broad potpourri of them and let the professionals arrange the mix for you. You could buy a country fund which has seen hard times, such as the Argentina Fund or the India Fund. There are also specific funds designated to this area such as Fidelity Emerging Markets, Montgomery Emerging Markets, and Vanguard International Index-Emerging.

For an aggressive investment in unproven territory, a mutual fund with its inherent diversification will act as a hedge against some of the risk.

Natalie is forty-two years old and married a second time. She has a son in high school. Her son is from her first marriage and she is partially responsible for his college education. She's an editor at a publishing company that is not publicly traded. She's been a client of mine for several years and already has in place a small personal account, an IRA, and a custodian account in her son's name and social security number (I will talk in detail about this kind of account in chapter 15). She called very excited to tell me she's taking a new job at another company.

"What do I do with my 401(k) plan at the old place?" she asked me.

"It's very simple," I answered. "We roll it right into your IRA. You won't have to pay any taxes now and all of it can continue to work tax-deferred for you."

"I'm getting a nice raise," she said. "Plus the new company's a public one so I'll start a stock purchase plan. I want to be aggressive now with this roll-over money."

Natalie told me she had close to $25,000 in her plan. She was a perfect candidate for a mixture of mutual funds. We had already made investments lessening the burden of her son's college tuition, and her IRA up until now was funded with low-risk tools. I suggested we put $5,000 in five different funds, working our way across the board from a growth fund, a growth and income fund, an international stock fund, one sector fund and one country fund.

By selecting a variety of funds, Natalie will be diversifying her assets even more while maintaining a certain control over her investment risk. She specified to me that she wanted to be more adventuresome. Another woman might choose a different posture. As I just demonstrated with Natalie, a portfolio can as easily be customized with mutual funds as it can be with individual stocks.

The mutual-fund path is the only path to consider for certain investors. The hands-off investor is one. If you have neither the time nor the inclination to follow your portfolio, to want to talk to your broker on some kind of regular basis, or to give her discretion, put your money in quality mutual funds.

Second, if you have very limited funds but can afford to leave this money invested for a period of years, a broad-spectrum mutual fund can easily be found to match your objectives.

Lastly, if you are keen to invest in the latest Wall Street exotica, modify that risk with a mutual fund purchase.

13

Investing Through Retirement Plans

RETIREMENT PLANS are an important element in your quest to build wealth. I am not going to discuss the pension or profit-sharing plans your company has set up for itself and its employees, because you are not in charge. Whether or not you are employed and whether or not your company provides for you, there are still other retirement plans that every woman qualifies for that should be utilized to the extent possible.

All personal retirement plans have some universal benefits:

1. They serve as a spur to savings.
2. They provide a built-in disciplined approach to your saving.
3. All contributions and investment returns whether in the form of gains or dividends and interest are accumulating for you tax deferred. Nothing is taxed to you until you start taking distributions from the plan.

In this chapter I will discuss IRAs, Keoghs and SEPs, 401(k)s and 403(b)s.

IRAs

An IRA, or Individual Retirement Account, is a tax-deferred retirement plan that you set up for yourself using pretax dollars.

When IRAs were originally conceived, you were able to deduct your annual contributions ($2,000 maximum) on your federal tax return. This deduction benefit was eliminated in l986, but as of this writing there is talk again in Washington of reviving it.

The IRA contribution still is a deductible expense, however, if you are *not* participating in a company retirement plan or if your adjusted gross income falls below certain limits.

Every year Vi asks me if she should fund her IRA even though the contribution isn't a deduction for her. Every year I tell her no. That's because Vi is one of my most organized and disciplined clients. She set up an IRA over twelve years ago and the original principal continues to work for her. More importantly, she maintains a personal account and has *never* once withdrawn any money from it. She is in a high tax bracket and likes income. In her personal account we concentrate on tax-free bonds. The tax-free interest she receives is worth more to her bottom line than tax-deferred investing without a tax deduction credit.

Her objectives haven't changed over the years, so each time she adds to her account, I continue to build on our original investments. Vi's retirement needs are met by her pension coverage at her job. Her net worth is expanding—mostly through the compounding of tax-free interest and dividends—in her brokerage account.

Cindy's situation is completely different. Like Vi she, too, is included in her company's pension plan, so any IRA contribution is not a deduction. Cindy cannot save, however. No sooner have we made a purchase in her personal account, than she calls me saying she needs some cash to see her through the month. Cindy should set up an IRA if for no other reason than it will force her to save. She would not be as tempted to withdraw from her IRA as she is from her personal account because she would pay a penalty for doing so any time before age 59½. And she's got a lot of years to go before she reaches that milestone!

The most common misconception about an IRA account is

that the IRA itself is a certain kind of investment. An IRA is purely a name designating this type of account from any other. It is held in your name with your social security number at either a bank, a mutual fund or insurance company, or at a brokerage firm. There is no one investment tool that has to go into your IRA. Your IRA may be as diversified as you wish. You may even have two IRAs running concurrently at both a mutual fund and at a brokerage firm.

Contrary to most women's first impression that only low-risk tools are desirable—especially considering that the IRA is for retirement purposes—is the fact that the younger you are and the sooner you start making contributions, the more growth oriented you can afford to be in your choice of investments. What is true for you personally, though, is as true in the IRA. No investment should be made simply on the basis of tax implications. Your risk-tolerance limits apply here as well. The fundamental truth is the younger you are when you start, the better!

My literary agent told me that her whole IRA is funded with zero coupon bonds. She has a guaranteed return and knows what her principal will be worth at an exact date in the future. Her husband only buys growth stocks and small company stocks in untested or more esoteric areas, i.e., gene replication and research. They both started with the same amount of money and his is now worth twice hers.

"Could you stand seeing your money go down once it reached a certain level?" I asked her.

"No."

"Does what's in your IRA keep you up at night?"

"I get the message," she said. "I'll stop complaining. I'd be a wreck if I had his portfolio."

If you are contributing to an IRA, whether or not the contribution is a deductible one, it pays to write that $2,000 check as early in the year as you can. That way you are getting the maximum advantage of the benefits of tax deferral because the money is invested longer.

Because the dollars you put into your IRA are pretax dollars, you are taxed at withdrawal time. If you take any withdrawal from an IRA before age 59½, you are subject both to ordinary income tax as well as a 10 percent penalty tax. Distributions rolled over from one IRA to another are not subject to tax as long as you don't receive the money personally. The transfer must be made directly from one institution to another.

Distributions may be taken free of penalty after age 59½ and are taxed as ordinary income when received. Distributions *must* begin by April 1 of the year in which you reach age 70½.

While the choices of investment for your IRA are wide-ranging, I have one particular strategy I recommend over all others. No matter how large or small the amount, I divide it in half. One half I put in zero coupon Treasury bonds. The other half I put in quality growth stocks. The zeros are the protection. The stocks give the nonguaranteed gain.

Let's use Tina as an example of how my strategy works. She's ready to make her very first IRA contribution. She has thirty years until retirement. Remember that a zero coupon bond is issued at a substantial discount from its face value of $1,000. Interest is not paid outright but is automatically reinvested, or compounded, at the rate that is stated when the bonds are purchased. Today, for half of her contribution, Tina could purchase five bonds locking in approximately a 6 percent yield. Translated into English, this means that if she doesn't touch this part of her investment, in thirty years her original $1,000 will be worth $5,000.

The second half I would put in a pure-growth mutual fund.

Margaret, as another example, had a long-term certificate of deposit come due at a bank. She rolled the entire $22,000 into a new brokerage IRA account. She told me she wanted to retire in ten years. The strategy doesn't change. Only the numbers do.

An $11,000 purchase today will buy about $19,000 worth of zero coupon Treasuries, at around a 5 percent yield, that mature in ten years. For the other $11,000 I would suggest a variety of blue chip stocks such as GE, Hewlett Packard, and Heinz, as well as a small investment in a higher-risk mutual fund, if Margaret were so inclined.

My strategy may not suit you or even your own broker. The more important issue is to have a strategy and to stick with it.

Keogh Plans

A *Keogh* plan is a retirement plan that is available to anyone who is self-employed or who has self-employment income outside of her regular income. For instance, I have a client who is employed by an advertising agency. She does free-lance work on her own time, however. The income derived from this outside work qualifies her for a Keogh.

The tax ramifications regarding a Keogh are the same as for an IRA, meaning that taxes on any gains or dividend income are deferred until you begin your withdrawal program. IRAs can be established up until April 15 for the previous year. Keoghs must be established *within* the tax year for which you intend to make contributions. You may make a token contribution, though, at inception time, $100 even, just to make the plan viable, and then make your full contribution at the time you file your tax return. Since Keoghs are larger plans, the IRS has different rules for them depending upon which type of Keogh you select.

The two most common forms of Keogh plans for a person making independent income and having no employees are a *profit-sharing plan* or a *money-purchase pension plan*. The former allows you to contribute and deduct up to the lesser of 13.04 percent of your self-employment income, or $30,000 into a profit-sharing plan. This plan is the more flexible because the contributions are made out of your profits and, therefore, are recalculated each year.

The money-purchase plan permits you to contribute and deduct up to the lesser of $30,000 or 20 percent of your self-employment income each year. You are putting away a larger percentage each year, but some flexibility is lost because the contributions are mandatory.

SEPs

A simplified employee pension (SEP) is a plan allowing an employer to make contributions toward an employee's retirement without having to set up a more complex retirement plan. If you are self-employed, you may contribute to your own SEP. In addition, even if your employer is contributing to a SEP for you, you can continue to maintain your own IRA.

The SEP rules permit an employer to make a deductible contribution each year to your SEP of up to 15 percent of your compensation but not more than $30,000. The rules are a little more complicated if you are self-employed. It would be best to talk to your tax adviser about calculating the exact amount.

The Keogh does require a tax return once it reaches a certain monetary size. The SEP does not. Also the SEP can be implemented after the December 31 deadline.

The withdrawal dates for all Keoghs and for SEPs are the same as for IRAs, as are the early withdrawal penalties.

My preferred strategy for investment does not change for these plans. With the larger sums available, you simply have more to work with to achieve accelerated growth and increase in principal. I would still put at least 25 percent in zero coupon bonds since they can always be purchased to correspond to the expected year of retirement. The known value at maturity can't be equaled for peace of mind. Maturities can also be selected to match your specific requirements for income once your retirement years have begun. The remaining monies can be allocated among a variety of investment tools according to both your income and growth goals.

401(k) Plans

The 401(k) plans are the hottest cards in the retirement account deck today. This particular pension program was instituted about fifteen years ago. Its pedestrian name actually comes from the IRS code that led to its creation.

A 401(k) is potentially the largest investment vehicle in the retirement arena. These tax-deferred plans, if available through your employer, provide distinct benefits, since they are the most significant retirement vehicle you can control yourself.

1. They allow you to set aside a portion of your salary on a pretax basis. This portion does not depend upon salary level. Automatic payroll deductions make this forced saving easy.
2. You are permitted to borrow against your plan. In paying back the loan, you are in essence paying interest to yourself. Remember, though, you are also losing the tax-free growth on the money you've borrowed.
3. You are usually offered a wide variety of investment options.
4. You can take advantage of averaging your cost basis because you are making systematic contributions of the same dollar amount to the same funds at regular intervals.
5. Your employer may match a portion of your contribution.

I am sure I am not in the minority when I say I have no faith that Social Security is going to be there for me during my retirement years—notwithstanding the fact that Social Security takes a bite out of every paycheck I get. The days when you would work for one company for a long time and then be rewarded at retirement by a comfortable pension are over. Pension and profit-sharing plans have been one of the casualties of corporate "reengineering" over the last decade.

If your company offers you a 401(k) plan, don't look at it as optional. As far as your retirement, it is a requirement, not an option. Most companies consider their 401(k) plan as an integral part of your overall employment/retirement package. It is up to you to take advantage of it. If you ignore this benefit, you'll have no one to blame but yourself when retirement time arrives.

The 401(k) is a relatively inexpensive way for companies to "help" their employees because there aren't the myriad of IRS regulations involved in pension-plan reporting and setup. The numbers speak for themselves. In the last five years, 401(k) assets have grown by 73 percent, while traditional corporate pensions have increased at less than half that rate. Under current law, you are eligible to invest up to 15 percent of your salary or a maximum of approximately $9,500 in 1996 in your 401(k) on a pretax basis (this amount is adjusted annually) depending upon inflation.

Unfortunately, the regulations for 401(k) plan standards are mostly voluntary. In fact, as I am writing this, there is an investigation going on by the Labor Department involving abuse of employees' funds. To safeguard yourself, use the following guidelines where applicable:

- The plan should offer you a minimum of three (or even five) investment choices of varying risk. You would ideally want to have a choice ranging through the whole risk spectrum from a low-risk money market fund all the way to an international equity fund.
- Assuming the employer is using a mutual fund company manager, the funds should be no-load or the no-load shares of load-fund families. Administrative and expense charges should be minimal.
- Account valuations should be easy to retrieve, and you should be able to move your money between investment funds at will—ideally with a phone call.
- You should be able to borrow up to as much as 50 percent of your plan. Your loan interest should be tied into the market rate of interest.
- Sometimes employers impose a one-year period of hire before participation is permitted. Look to see if you can start contributions immediately, and pay attention to the percentage your employer will match.

If you have a personal account at a brokerage firm, run the investment choices by your broker that your employer gives you for your 401(k) plan. It makes sense for you to check with your broker for two reasons. One is that she probably will be more familiar with the instruments you're to pick from and two, she can work those choices into your entire investment plan.

Even though the 401(k) is outside the traditional brokerage purview, it still is part of your investment pie. Renee has a $100,000 brokerage account with me. She'd never mentioned her 401(k) plan until last month. Her employer was widening the web of available investments and she wanted my advice. Her retirement plan at work is now worth close to $50,000. When she spoke to me about it, I realized we should do some restructuring in her personal account.

Renee is in her mid-thirties, but her retirement plan has built up this far because she's worked at the same company for ten years. She is unmarried and has no deductions. I advised her to put a combination of high-yield and more aggressive growth tools in her 401(k) plan. Neither the dividends nor the capital gains would be currently taxed to her. We would go for longer-term growth in her personal account and switch to some tax-free municipal bonds. (It's unnecessary to buy tax-frees in a retirement plan because the money that accumulates is already tax deferred.)

Another self-defeating strategy is to blindly allocate all, or a large percentage, of the money in your 401(k) to buying your own company's stock. You may work for the best company in the world by your and every other financial and socially conscious standard. There is just too much risk to owning too much of any one stock—even the stock of the company you work for. Buy the stock instead through the privileged employee stock-purchase plan. This way you are buying at a discount and the percentage amount is automatically deducted from your paycheck.

The 401(k) plan is offering you another opportunity for asset allocation. Use this opportunity. Don't ever put all the proverbial eggs in one basket.

When and if the day comes when you and this terrific company may decide you're both not so terrific for each other anymore, your 401(k) can still say a tax-deferred *adios* along with you. It is possible to leave your funds at your old job until retirement, but since there are other available avenues, I can't see why anyone would want to do so.

One option is to move the plan to your new employer. You would, of course, have to liquidate your positions and just transfer cash. Make sure this transfer is done by what is called a trustee-to-trustee form to avoid tax penalties. You might choose this option if the new plan's investment choices are much better than those of the one you are leaving, and if you want the simplicity and convenience of having your 401(k) in one place.

Some firms will not accept a transfer and some make you wait until you have been employed a year. Also, you may decide that you want even more control over your own money. In that case you can roll over your plan's proceeds into your brokerage or mutual fund company IRA account also without tax penalty. You and your broker can then make your own independent selections from the broadest possible choices.

Being fifty-something has its own special advantage. If you are at least fifty-five and you change jobs, you can cash out your existing 401(k) plan and you won't incur a tax penalty.

A *403(b) plan* is a particular type of retirement plan sponsored only by certain not-for-profits such as religious, charitable, or public education organizations. These plans are significantly smaller and the organization doesn't invest itself. It sends the employee contribution directly to a so-designated brokerage account. The money never passes through the employees' hands. In my experience, the amount may be as little as $1,000 and is only paid once a year. Still, take what you can get. Any money in a 403(b) will give you a tax benefit.

Depending upon your life situation, you may find that you want to utilize every retirement plan device you possibly can. Lila, the interior decorator, and her lawyer husband Robert found this to be the case. Their combined taxable income today is over $250,000 and their federal tax bracket of 39.6 percent forces them to constantly reexamine how they save and how they invest. They both have IRAs, although Robert has not contributed to his since 1987 when he lost the tax deduction benefit. Robert has been participating in his law firm's 401(k) for at least fifteen years. Lila told me they felt they still needed some supplemental retirement protection. It was time to talk to her about a tax-deferred annuity.

14

Investing Through Tax-Deferred Annuities

AN ANNUITY IS A CONTRACT between you and an insurance company. In some sort of financial irony, however, an annuity is also the *opposite* of insurance. Insurance protects your family and/or your beneficiaries from financial hardship in the event of your premature demise. An annuity, in contrast, helps continue your financial security in the event you live longer than life expectancy tables predict you will.

Even though investing in an annuity, by definition, means investing in an insurance product, I am not going to explore any other kind of insurance vehicles. A deferred annuity is a wealth-building instrument. Traditional insurance is a protective device.

One doesn't buy an annuity in joint name. Lila and Robert decided Lila would buy the annuity in her own name. Their two children would be the beneficiaries. Most policies have a minimum purchase amount of $5,000. Lila and Robert had $25,000 segregated that they decided to use as a lump-sum purchase. They are also allowed to make subsequent contributions of any amount.

Annuities have the same tax-deferred investing benefits of an IRA, Keogh, 401(k), or 403(b) (see preceding chapter). You should continue to take advantage of the smaller plans first because some of those dollars may be pretax dollars and because these vehicles generate lower expenses than do some kinds of annuities.

What annuities have in their favor is no cap on the amount you are allowed to invest. The mandatory withdrawal age is also higher. Some annuities allow you to postpone withdrawals until age eighty-five.

We have explored earlier the benefits of tax-deferred investing. I need to emphasize again, however, the importance of the maxim, the earlier, the better. The sooner you start your retirement planning, the longer your money has to work for you. That's one reason to start with the smaller plans. You won't be jeopardizing your need for liquidity. Investing in an annuity should come last, because even though you may get a charge out of the thought of putting one over on Uncle Sam with this heftier contribution, the withdrawal penalties remain severe. The IRS exacts the same taxes, the 10 percent penalty is in effect for the accumulated earnings before age $59\frac{1}{2}$, and you can expect to pay a surrender charge.

Lila and Robert have no liquidity problems. And at Lila's age, she can still look forward to a good thirty years of tax-deferred compounding. The "rule of ten" says that money invested at 10 percent doubles in seven years. Although there are no promises, I couldn't totally prevent visions of dollar signs dancing in their heads.

The next decision they'd have to make is whether to buy a fixed or a variable annuity. A *fixed-rate annuity* is designed to provide a predictable rate of return. A fixed interest rate for a specified period of time—generally one year—is declared and guaranteed by the issuing insurance company at the time of the annuity's purchase. At the end of the initial rate guarantee period, the company will declare a new interest rate that is based on both the current interest rate environment as well as the performance of the company's underlying investment portfolio. This same pattern will occur every year.

The company will also impose a charge on money withdrawn during the early years of the contract. The surrender charge customarily starts at 7 percent and declines to no charge year by year during a seven-year or so period.

If you are contemplating a fixed annuity, investigate the following:

1. What is the insurance company's financial strength? You want to make sure it has the capability to invest and safeguard your money.
2. What is the insurance company's rating and credit history? Has the company consistently paid reasonable and competitive rates to its annuity holders?
3. What are the specific surrender charges?
4. What are the conditions, if any, under which you can withdraw money without a penalty?

The fixed annuity probably is the better choice for the very conservative investor. The woman who is more likely to stick with certificates of deposit, short-term bonds, and income stocks is more likely to feel comfortable with the kind of annuity which gives her a predetermined rate of return rather than one whose value will fluctuate with market conditions.

The benefits of a *fixed-rate annuity* are:

- a specific minimum rate of return is guaranteed
- the insurance company assumes the investment risk
- when you annuitize (receive payments), the payments are a specified amount for the contract term.

I felt that Lila would want a variable annuity, but I had to make sure she understood the differences between the fixed and variable type. A *variable annuity* involves more work on the investor's part, but the rate of return ought to make the work worthwhile. In a variable annuity, your money is invested in professionally managed portfolios of stocks, bonds, or both. The rate of return is not guaranteed. It will fluctuate with changes in the equities markets. If the return potential is met, a variable can also reduce the risk of inflation eating away part of the return.

A variable annuity is as much an insurance policy as is the fixed annuity. Under the variable, however, each policy, or contract, offers a variety of funds, often referred to as subaccounts, in which you can invest. These fund options should include a stock fund, a bond fund, a high-grade or government fund, a money market fund, and even some foreign or specialty portfolios. A prospectus is provided with any mutual fund purchase. Study this prospectus because you are making your own investment decisions. You want to do the homework necessary to be sure you are not taking on more risk than you can handle.

I say there's more work involved, because if you are conscientious you can maintain control of this investment. Depending upon your own financial goals, you may allocate and reallocate your money among the different available funds by paying attention to shifting economic conditions.

A subaccount's performance is tracked by the *accumulation unit value* (AUV). The AUV is not unlike the NAV of a mutual fund. It is not a figure you can get to yourself. First the change in the value of the investment has to be measured. Then the portfolio's income and realized capital gains are added. Lastly, management and insurance expenses are subtracted.

Variable annuities generally require relatively small initial investments (i.e., $5,000) and permit flexible, additional deposits. While there is no front-end sales charge, meaning that whatever you contribute goes to work for you right then and there, you will still face surrender fees. These fees tend to run higher than those for fixed annuities and decline over a longer span of years.

There are other expenses. In annuity lingo, these expenses are referred to as the "wrapper." The main insurance cost is the "mortality and expense" charge, the "M&E." This is the percentage of the annuity's assets that the insurance company deducts to insure the guaranteed death benefit. M&E charges can run from as little as .50 to 1.4 percent.

The guaranteed death benefit insures that, in the event of

your death, the policy will be worth at least as much as you contributed.

There is usually also an administrative fee and there could be an extra fee for enhanced guarantees. Cumulatively, according to The *VARDS Report,* a publication that tracks variable annuities, fees can run a bit over 2 percent. Bottom line: that's why you want to be involved in managing your account. You've got to cover those fees—a very do-able job if you pay attention.

If you are buying an annuity on your own and not through a financial adviser, you may want to read one issue of *VARDS*. You can write to Box 1927, Roswell, Georgia 30077-1927, or call (770) 998-5186.

The same goes for Morningstar, the number one name in mutual fund rating. Morningstar reports on variable annuities as well. The telephone number is (800) 876-5005.

Lila and Robert could talk to me about tax-deferred annuities because I am insurance registered and because my firm offers a wide variety of variable annuities. Since annuities combine attributes of both securities and insurance, one must be licensed in both fields in order to sell them. You will have to ask your stockbroker if she is insurance licensed and if her firm deals in that area.

You can also buy annuities from many mutual fund groups that sell directly to the public without sales people as intermediaries. Vanguard, Scudder, and Fidelity are some of the names. The large insurance companies such as Lincoln National Life, Hartford Life, and The Travelers, as you would expect, deal heavily in annuities. These insurance companies, however, conduct business through a brokerage house or mutual fund family.

No matter who is making the decision on the variable annuity, either you alone or you with your stockbroker, this is what you will want to know:

1. How wide-ranging are the investment choices?
2. What are the track records for the particular funds?
3. Are there any outstanding features of that annuity? For

example, how easy will it be to move from fund to fund? Can your stockbroker do it for you? Do you have to call the fund yourself? And, is there an 800 number?
4. What are the annual expenses or charges?

The second phase of a deferred annuity is the annuitization phase. When you decide to withdraw, to annuitize, you are making an *irrevocable* decision. Ordinarily the owner and the annuitant are one and the same. This does not have to be, but the payouts are always based on the life of the owner/annuitant. There are several forms of payout annuity options, but each should be looked at as a case-by-case situation. Talk to your tax adviser about the right option for you.

Payouts can be structured to meet various planning needs and three different parties need to be considered: the owner, the annuitant (or the payee), and the beneficiary. All payouts, however, have a preferential tax treatment.

A portion of each monthly payment is tax-free. That is because a portion of each payment represents a return of your original principal payment. This portion is called the exclusion amount and is reached by dividing the amount of the original investment by the expected number of payments. The balance of each monthly check is taxed as ordinary income as it is received.

The benefits of a *variable annuity* are:

- Unlimited rate of return potential but no guaranteed minimum rate
- You as the owner assume the investment risk but also can reap greater reward
- When you annuitize, the payments are variable at regular intervals for the contract term.

All *annuities* have the following benefits:

- significant tax advantages—tax deferral of all earnings; compound interest
- no up-front sales charge

- loan value
- variety of payout options
- guaranteed income options
- no probate involved—the proceeds of an annuity are paid directly to your named beneficiary bypassing public probate procedures.

15

Ages Twenty-Five to Thirty-Nine

YOU HAVE DONE YOUR MATH HOMEWORK. You have learned about the investment tools, and you have made some decisions about your retirement money. It is time now to act. What precisely do you want to invest in at various time spans of your life? Which investments are optimum when?

Each life stage has its own goals. Some of those goals, as we have discussed amply, will modify depending upon your risk-tolerance. Other goals will depend upon your individual situation—for instance, are you single, married, have children, have dependent parents, need to save for college tuitions, want to retire early, and so on?

Let us look at various scenarios within three broad life cycles. I'll talk about real women and the investment concerns they face within these time frames. I'll offer my own investment advice on how best to meet these challenges and concerns.

This first cycle is the time when it is the most important not only to invest but to invest for long-term growth. Unfortunately, this cycle is also the time when you probably have the least amount of cash to devote to your investments. Mother Time is on your side, however. Certainly she is when it comes to retirement planning. The small contribution multiplies greatly over a thirty- or even forty-year period. Your short-term (less than a year) and even your intermediate term goals may be more difficult to accomplish because of the lack of sufficient savings.

Stephanie, Single, Age 27
Short-term goal: liquidity
Medium-term goal: buy a new car at end of lease period
Long-term goal: start preparing for retirement

Stephanie has just received her doctorate. She has just accepted a job with a different firm. She's received a raise, but the job involved relocating to a city with a significantly higher cost of living. She anticipates that her remaining cash after paying her monthly expenses will be pretty much what it is now despite the higher salary. She owes no money. She rents her apartment and her car is on a three-year lease.

Stephanie is lucky enough to have me as her mother, so she was raised to be disciplined about money and budgeting! This is something I urge every one of you to do with your own children. Learning money management at a mother's knee is a skill which cannot be duplicated.

Now that she is earning her own paycheck, Stephanie wants to be responsible for her money and to create wealth for herself. When she called me to say she had $5,000 that she didn't need for monthly expenses, but still wanted to keep available for emergencies or shorter-term needs, I suggested she check the rates for a six-month certificate of deposit at some of her local banks. A banker is always a good person to know for a financial reference and I wanted to get her used to talking about an investment vehicle with someone else.

Her first attempts at retirement planning were somewhat aborted. The first company she worked for was not a public one but did offer her participation in a 401(k) plan after she had been working there for six months. The plan was only worth about $100 when she left this company and the new company didn't allow a transfer. For this tiny amount, I suggested she simply withdraw it and pay her taxes.

She will restart a 401(k) plan as soon as she is eligible. If she contributes as little as $100 monthly, using the most conservative estimate of an 8 percent rate of return, in forty years her 401(k) will be worth $351,428. If she averages a 12 percent rate of return over forty years, the same $100 per month will climb to $1,188,242. Because her second employer is a public company, she'll participate as well in the employee stock-purchase program.

She's rolled over her CD once already and added some to the principal. By the time it comes due again, she will see if she has been able to save money in her new surroundings. With the existing certificate and whatever additions she will be able to make over time, she should be able to afford the car she wants to buy.

Anita, Single, Age 31
Short-term goal: pay her bills
Medium-term goal: buy a condo
Long-term goal: buy an airplane

Anita is probably more recognizable than Stephanie. She is not quite finished paying off the last of her student loans, although she has been working full time for a few years as a pilot for Delta Airlines. She's maxed out on her credit cards. Still she manages to buy the newest compact disk each week. She has tried every deal Sprint, MCI, or AT&T can offer but even Candy Bergen can't tone down her phone bills.

Anita has a bit of catch-up work to do. Her goals may look slightly ridiculous at first glance. When I heard her reasoning, however, I became more of a believer and decided to try to help.

Anita's salary is $40,000. She wasn't putting anything away either in a retirement plan or in Delta's stock-purchase program. I couldn't persuade her to participate in a 401(k) because she insisted she wasn't going to stay at Delta that long and didn't want to have to deal with transferring the plan. I finally got her to agree to set up an IRA account for herself at my firm. If she would send me what she paid for her weekly CD, that is, about $17, or $68 a month, in four months time I'd have the $250 minimum necessary to start a mutual fund purchase for her.

Each time her contributions reached $100, I could reinvest. These amounts sound minuscule, and it might seem like a lot of work for nothing on both our parts, but that really isn't true. I felt the effort was worth it to teach her about disciplined saving and the power of dollar-cost investing.

Dollar-cost averaging means you do not invest all of your money at once—even if you have a larger amount available to invest. The dollar cost of the fund Anita will be buying will change over time. Since she is investing $100 each time, she will sometimes be paying higher prices and buying few shares. Conversely, when the price is lower, she will be purchasing more shares. Over time, the average cost of the shares will almost always be lower than the average price.

The terms of her student loan were quite lenient but it was time to curtail some of her self-indulgent spending and get those loans out of the way.

I was not certain that she would have the money to buy a condo in roughly seven years. If she stayed on course, though, and if interest rates stayed low enough, she might be in good enough financial shape. If the airline industry stayed healthy as well, she expected her paycheck to increase accordingly.

Now for the airplane. The idea wasn't as flaky as it seemed at first. Anita explained to me that for about half a million dollars she'd be able to buy a used, but serviceable small jet. She planned to start her own business as an independent contractor who leased out her time to various corporations. She had done enough research on the proposal to convince me. The plane was not a whimsy. It was the means to a viable long-term economic future for her to set up her own company. She would then be able to provide for more of her own retirement needs once she was in business.

Laurel, Single, Age 37
Short-term goal: save money
Medium-term goal: make some money
Long-term goal: save on taxes

If the above goals look both familiar but vague to you, don't worry. They do to me too. What Laurel wants is what every woman wants, but these are not specific goals. In fact, one or more of these wishes will dominate during evolving cycles in your life, but this kind of wish does not translate into being able to set a financial plan. The irony is that Laurel works for a financial institution and earns $75,000. She has access to almost as much information as I do, but I myself cannot get her to focus on her own account. She is a New Jersey resident and after repeated conversations I got her to buy a New Jersey short-term municipal bond. The balance of her $50,000 portfolio languishes in a money market account.

What is true is that she will not lose money—or she won't unless inflation should reappear and eat away at her money market interest. She isn't making money either. She is still young enough to invest in a more growth-oriented direction. If she finds pure growth too risky, she could buy a balanced mutual fund or a stock that has a high dividend return.

The interest she is receiving from her New Jersey bond is tax-free. This small amount is not enough to make an impact on her tax return.

She is covered by a pension plan at the insurance company where she is employed, and I am afraid she is being unrealistic about what Social Security is actually going to be paying her in thirty years. Unless Laurel wakes up to her situation, she is going to be one of those who unfortunately find themselves significantly less comfortable financially during retirement than they were during their wage-earning years.

Debra and Jim, Newlyweds, Ages 29 and 33
Short-term goal: start an investment program
Medium-term goal: buy a house and have children
Long-term goal: retire to Florida or Arizona

Debra's parents gave her a good financial background. She's also a trust and estate lawyer and earns $80,000. She began contributing to her own individual retirement account while still in law school. She does not make further contributions now because she participates in her firm's 401(k) plan. She told me that the firm matches half of her contributions up to 3 percent of her salary. While she and Jim are still childless, I strongly suggested she put into the plan the maximum amount. She may have to reduce that amount later on when family expenses increase, but she would be getting a solid foundation.

Jim is a physical therapist for recovering heart attack patients at a local hospital. His salary at $30,000 is much less than hers— as it will continue to be in the future. They use his health benefits, however, and as long as he is employed at the hospital, their medical care costs should be reduced as well as being quite accessible. Jim also has adequate insurance and retirement coverage through his job. They are currently living in a condo partially subsidized by the hospital, so housing expenses are less than they would be in other circumstances.

Debra and Jim do not need current income. They want to see their assets increase in value. Debra told me they had worked out a plan and decided they could put aside $200 a month for investment purposes.

I suggested to her that they segregate that money in a separate bank account or even mentally in their checkbook until they reached $1,500. That would take just seven and a half months. With $1,500 I could start a money market account for them. In the meantime, I would be sending them information on various growth-oriented mutual funds, and they would have time to study the prospectuses while they were accumulating the minimum necessary. Once the money market was open, Debra could send the $200 directly to me each month, and each time we reached $500, we would reinvest or make a new investment.

As Debra's salary grew, she would be able to send more in each month. They had made the decision to live as frugally as necessary, until they were ready to have children, in order to start building an investment program as soon as possible. Then, during the years that they could not contribute in this same substantive way, the plan they had funded earlier would still be working for them to meet their longer-term objectives.

Debra was aware she could borrow against her 401(k) in the future should she want to when they were ready to buy a house. That was not a decision we needed to make now. It probably would make more sense to borrow against some of their portfolio (go on margin) or even to liquidate some holdings if necessary. It does not make sense to make those predictions now. Portfolio performance, the interest-rate climate, the direction of the economy and the amount of money they'd need would all have to be measured when the time was appropriate.

Marisa and Evan, Parents of a Two-Year-Old, Both 35
Short-term goal: not go into debt
Medium-term goal: prepare for college tuition
Long-term goal: pay off mortgage before retirement

Marisa and Evan met at a fund-raising political event, got married six months later and bought a house for $150,000, and had a baby within the next year. Evan is a legislative aide to their state senator and Marisa freelances as a speechwriter. The house needs fixing up but Evan is handy and enjoys that kind of work. They only put down 15 percent of the purchase price so their mortgage payments are relatively high at $870 per month, although the interest deduction is helpful on their tax return. Evan's health plan covers the family. His state pension is their only other investment.

Marisa has frequent assignments and does her writing at home. I reminded her to keep careful records. She may be able to write off a portion of their payments because she has a bona fide office right in the house. The thought of putting any of her speechwriting money into an illiquid IRA made her too uneasy. She and Evan preferred to keep up-to-date on their mortgage payments and even prepay them when possible. They knew they would have to change the lifestyles they enjoyed as singles by buying this house but they were willing to make the adjustment. And they looked upon the house as a form of investment as well.

As we explored their goals further, it turned out that their baby son had received birthday money that was sitting in a bank savings account. When Marisa checked the passbook, she was surprised to see it was as much as $1,000. I strongly recommended that she and Evan not put funding their son's education off as a medium-term goal. One thousand dollars invested in a zero coupon bond today would bring them $3,000 by the time he was in college. Remember from our earlier discussion of zero coupon Treasuries, that one of the big pluses about this kind of investment is that from inception you know exactly how much your money is going to be worth at maturity.

In this investment, Marisa wouldn't be facing the illiquidity of an IRA account. It is not mandatory to hold a zero until the due date. Any zero can be sold at current market value at will. It is also not necessary to liquidate an entire position. If she needed a certain amount of money for a specific purpose, she could sell only enough to satisfy that amount.

Marisa and Evan need to open a custodian account for their son. This type of account accomplishes two purposes: 1) the account is identified by the youngster's Social Security number and is therefore taxed at his lower tax bracket and not that of his parents', and 2) it is a mechanism for building wealth to meet his own future expenses.

This type of account is established by the *Uniform Gifts to Minors Act* (UGMA). The account is simple to set up. Either parent is custodian (not both) for the child and the child's Social Security number is used. The only potential drawback is that when the child becomes eighteen, the account legally may become his upon presentation of proof of age. In most cases this is no problem. The account is used for college tuition as originally planned and payments are made out of it accordingly.

The unfortunate news is that if your child is turning out to be a "bad egg," you are still stuck with this account. You could always send the child to military school at age thirteen, use the money to pay the tuition, and hope you get your money's worth! Setting up a trust instead of a UGMA account is the only way to keep your child from claiming the money at age eighteen.

Zeros are one ideal investment for a UGMA account because the increments in value are not that much each year. If you have greater amounts to put away for your children, you do want to be aware of the "kiddie tax." Until your child is fourteen, any unearned income in excess of $1,200 is taxed at the parents' rate. You want to keep the earnings below that level. There are several ways besides zeros to keep the income low. You can buy tax-free bonds in that account. Tax-free interest doesn't apply. You can buy growth stocks or growth mutual funds. Let these securities appreciate in value over the years and postpone their sale until the child reaches age fourteen. Then the gains are taxed at the child's own lower rate.

Marisa and Evan would keep themselves from borrowing; they did not want to owe any money over and above the mortgage. They agreed that the best way for them to save was to funnel any money they could into their son's custodian account. This way they would be working on all of their goals at once. And if Marisa's freelance work became more active in the future, they would have extra money to use to plan for the long term.

Fran and Mark, Second Marriage for Both, Son 6 Years Old, Ages 38 and 51
Short-term goal: save on taxes
Medium-term goal: their son's college tuition
Long-term goal: retirement and travel

Fran works in the development office of a museum. She makes $40,000. She has a twelve-year-old daughter from her first marriage who lives with her and Mark. Under the divorce agreement, her former husband is responsible for his daughter's schooling. Because of this, she receives no child support. Fran told me that her former husband is a stockbroker. He had done the right planning for them using a custodian account from the start, and she was hopeful she could meet any necessary supplementing.

Mark, a graphics designer at a computer company, has a son already out of college. They have a small mortgage on their apartment and one car fully paid for. Mark's been participating in a 401(k) plan for over twelve years. I reviewed his investment choices with him and we made some switches to more growth-oriented funds. He had no thoughts of taking an early retirement so there was no need to use a shortened investment horizon. There are rumors that his company may go public, which would be a real windfall for him.

Fran participates in a 403(b) at the museum, but the compounding of her retirement account is not remarkable because of the small amounts that are allowed as contributions each year. They are in the highest tax bracket and would like more tax-advantaged investments.

She had opened a custodian account at her bank and had about $10,000 in a two-year CD for her son which would be coming due in a couple of months. This amount had grown thanks to the $1,000 that his grandparents gave him each year on his birthday.

I recommended that Fran transfer this account to my firm when the CD came due and we buy zero coupon bonds with the principal plus the birthday money for this year. We'd be at least able to double his money and I thought the best thing would be to divide the total into four pieces. I could buy zeros to mature during each of the four college years. As he received more gift money, and as Fran and Mark found that they could add to his account, we would build sequentially on each piece.

Fran and Mark live in Manhattan—a high-tax state and city. With their personal account, I suggested we focus on tax-advantaged investments rather than setting up another retirement plan. There are several Nuveen New York insured or high-quality closed-end bond funds. These stocks are traded on the NYSE and they pay monthly interest at approximately a 5.5 percent tax-free rate. This translates into over an 8 percent comparable taxable return. The monthly interest could be swept into a money market fund and more shares could be bought systematically. Should they ever need money, any number of shares can be sold and the proceeds available in three business days.

If Mark's company were to go public, the options he held would be converted to public shares. We would have to do some serious tax planning at that time. Right now it is necessary to plan for what they have—not for what they hope to have.

We can see from all these examples that no situation is the same but no objective is so very different from another. As a young adult woman, you are coming into your own professionally at this stage. You want to achieve the best that you can for yourself financially as well. You may find yourself in a quandary about some of your goals. If you are single, should you buy a condo or should you stay unencumbered and rent? If you are newly married, should you save for your anticipated family? Do you really have to think about retirement your first day on the job?

The only certain answer is probably yes to the last question. You should not get yourself in a position where you owe more money than you are taking in. It is okay to borrow for a mortgage. It is not okay to borrow against your credit card for too many frivolous purchases.

It is never too early to start to plan how to keep the money you make. While professional, career, marital or family demands all can appear to be uppermost at any given time, each woman must decide for herself how much she can afford to have deducted from her paycheck or how much she can put away herself to meet her own investment objectives.

To accomplish all that, it is important to keep your finances as flexible as possible so that you can reposition yourself for emerging opportunities or unexpected changes.

Three key investment goals for women aged twenty-five to thirty-nine should be:

- asset growth
- provision for anticipated tuitions
- early preparation for retirement.

16

Ages Forty to Fifty-Four

THESE FIFTEEN YEARS encompass an investment period when a woman can financially and psychologically afford the most risk.

Generally these years represent a combination of high wage earning, a paid-up or close-to-being-paid-up mortgage, college tuition that is more a memory than a looming obstacle, and a career peak. As another woman once said to me, she felt as if she had gotten a huge raise once she had finished paying for her kids' college education. All of a sudden there was a lot more money in her bank account.

On the other hand, you may be part of a second family and education funding is still ahead of you. Perhaps you also have elderly and infirm parents. You may find yourself divorced in the middle of your fortieth decade and feel both fearful and resentful that you must revisit the financial concerns of a single person.

You might also be single again because you have been prematurely widowed. You are nervous about your financial situation and outlook. These are legitimate concerns that must be addressed.

This second cycle—which theoretically should be the most productive—may instead be more worrisome financially than those behind you if you have not planned accordingly. This is a period when the misconception that you are invulnerable really becomes a misconception.

There are some financial fundamentals particularly relevant

to this age cycle. Assuming you have started to build a certain degree of wealth, there are protective devices you need to be aware of that prevent Uncle Sam from taking more of his due.

- Make sure you (and your husband) have an up-to-date will.
- If you are married, you are doing yourself a disservice to insist all property should be in joint name.
- If you are divorced, remember *alimony* is fully taxable to you; *child support* is not reportable income on your tax return.
- If your parents need financial support from you, you may, under certain circumstances, claim them as dependents.

Even though I mention having a will as number one on the list, I am not going to delve into the intricacies of estate planning in this book. *Estate planning* exists to preserve and protect your estate. It is concerned with the transferring of your assets and making sure the liquidity is there to effect this transfer as well as pay your taxes.

This book is about financial planning. *Financial planning* is making these assets grow. A will belongs under both topics because the will is your means of taking control over who gets the assets you have accumulated. There's no sense in working hard to build wealth and then die intestate (which means, without a will). You build wealth to take care of yourself but also to take care of those you love. Do not think of a will as something referring to death. A will protects those who live after you. It can be the exclamation mark that completes the story of your life. Why should your state government's tax code determine who gets what and in what percentage? Let your assets continue to grow in the hands of your beneficiaries after your death.

The subject of joint ownership has many twists and turns. Pure and simple, for the sake of independence (forgetting about taxes for the minute), keep everything in your single name. Your will facilitates the distribution of property to anyone you name.

Here is something most women do not know, however. Remember when we talked about self-deferred annuities, I said an annuity passed directly to the beneficiary without having to go through the court probate process. Well, so does a brokerage account if it is held in joint name. The exact title is *Joint Tenant With Right of Survivorship* (JTWROS). You can be joint tenant with *anyone* you select—a husband, a child, a parent, a friend. The account is identified for IRS purposes with either person's Social Security number. At your death the account goes automatically to the other owner.

This happens in reverse as well. If the other person who is "joint" on the account with you dies before you, you inherit the account without passing through probate. *A joint account supersedes the will.* Even if you direct in your will that your brokerage account is to go to your children and your husband's name is on the account with yours, the account *must* go to your husband. If you are the sole name on the account, the account's disposition will follow what is written in your will.

A brokerage account is the *only* piece of property I recommend having in joint name with any other person. This time I am not talking as a feminist but as an adviser who wants you to keep all the money you can out of the IRS's clutches. The marital deduction is a major tax saver.

You can will to your husband (and he can will to you) as much as either of you want and neither your nor his estate will pay gift or estate tax. This postponement only works until the second of you dies. Then the property will be taxed in the surviving spouse's estate—*unless* you've been totally financially responsible and talked to an estate lawyer or accountant. There are insurance arrangements, marital deduction trusts, and marital deduction trusts with charitable remainders which can ensure that a great percentage of your property will remain intact and go, without severe tax penalties, exactly where you (and your spouse) want it to go.

Divorce is seldom a time for celebration. Retribution is a more normal response, and what better way to get even than to ask for a lot of alimony. Your ex-to-be may be more than happy to pay you the alimony. That is a tax deduction for him on money that is fully taxable to you. Again, talk to a tax adviser, but, if you have children, think about receiving support for them rather than for you.

What is definitely likely to happen is that you will find yourself with increased costs post-divorce. Two do live cheaper than one. You will probably have to readjust your spending and construct a whole new expense worksheet. If you have not been working full-time, you may find yourself back in the job market and reviewing your holdings in order to supplement income.

The good news about having to support your parents may be that you can claim some of that support as a deduction. The bad news is that you have to find ways to fund that support. Let's stick with the good news for the time being.

You may claim your parent(s) as a dependent on your income tax return if your parent meets a set of criteria, some of which are easy to fulfill, such as: 1) he or she does not file a joint income tax return; 2) he or she is a U.S. citizen or resident of the United States, Canada, or Mexico; 3) more than half of the support for the year is provided by you.

The most difficult requirement is the one stating that his or her gross income must be less than the personal exemption amount for that particular year. In 1995, the amount was $2,500. As you can see, the amount is small. You will have to go over a parent's finances very carefully to make sure that that amount is not exceeded. Again, see a tax adviser if you find you need to rechannel some of the income to make sure you are doing it legally.

Another method is to get your parent to pay for all her expenses first until she is "broke." This can be a very difficult concept to get an elderly person to accept but if she does not have assets, she will not be receiving any income either, and she will qualify as a dependent.

With or without the dependency exemption, and assuming you yourself have the money to do so, you can pay your parent's medical bills as long as you pay the medical expenses *directly* to the health care provider. If these expenses vault over 7.5 percent of your adjusted gross income, you can take the deduction even if they are on someone's behalf and not on yourself.

Let's look at some specific examples and see how these women found the answers to their own middle-cycle financial dilemmas. It will look somewhat repetitious but *every* woman at this stage says she is worried about having enough money set aside for her retirement needs. For some women it is even a short-term goal. For others it still seems farther off.

These women are right to be concerned about retirement. The problem is not all of them are doing anything about it. I think women and men are voicing these concerns but somehow think the genie is coming to appear at the last minute to save them. I say this because of the results of a recent Yankelovich survey I heard on the *Nightly Business Report*.

Men and women were not differentiated in the survey, but I am reasonably sure the information is not gender-specific. A good 25 percent of those questioned said they were not saving for retirement. Those who were investing were putting their savings in cash or certificates of deposit. Yet a strong majority of those surveyed felt secure about their retirement.

Something is very askew in both the thinking and acting about retirement. First of all, if you aren't saving, you aren't going to have the money to retire on. Second, as I've illustrated earlier, investing in purely cash and low-risk investments, unless you are already in the retirement state, just is not going to keep up with inflation over time and produce the results you expect. And, lastly, who's being the ostrich here? How can one feel secure without making provisions?

Clearly everyone is *thinking* about retirement. Very few are *doing* anything about it, however. My goal is to make sure my clients do plan for retirement.

Betsy, Single, Age 43
Short-term goal: reduce taxes
Medium-term goal: plan for retirement
Long-term goal: be able to travel overseas frequently

Betsy is a television movie producer now earning $125,000. She started her career at Home Box Office and worked there ten years. She has several thousand shares of Time Warner stock in her personal account, which she purchased as an employee at a discount from today's market price. She also had close to $100,000 in a 401(k) which she rolled over into an IRA. She now works for an independent, private company and is covered by that company's own pension and profit-sharing plan.

She has very few deductions. She owns a condo and her mortgage is almost paid up. She has never married and has no dependents. She travels constantly for business purposes and is completely involved in her own career. She wanted to put a plan into motion that would be self-perpetuating and she was willing to give me discretion to make changes when they were warranted.

The first thing we did was convert her personal account into a check-writing one with a cash card attached. Betsy would pay her tax estimates and any other large bill directly from this account. Her accountant received copies of all her brokerage transactions, and would be able to see the paper trail of any checks she wrote that qualified as tax deductions, e.g. the payment of her state taxes as a deduction on her federal return.

Betsy would also have immediate access to cash when she was on the road if an emergency occurred. Third, she arranged for her company to make a direct deposit of her paycheck into her brokerage account. She felt she would be much better at saving that way. She would pay herself an "allowance" each month from this account and transfer that amount to her bank checking account for her living expenses.

She had not thought much about individual stocks in the past because her portfolio was top-heavy with Time Warner stock. She had placed the rest of her cash, about $50,000, into certificates of deposit just to do something with it so she did not have to be bothered with any other money decisions.

For the time being, I advised keeping the Time Warner stock. She would have a large capital gain to pay on any sales, and entertainment stocks are in play. When the certificate of deposit came due, I suggested we move into Massachusetts tax-free bonds of five- to seven-year maturities. Betsy was receiving 5 percent interest fully taxable on her CD. The Massachusetts munis would give her about 4.5 percent completely tax-free instead—a much better bottom-line return.

We also decided on a minimum balance to perpetuate in her money market account. Every time that balance had $5,000 or more surplus, I would make a quality growth-stock investment. This way her net worth would increase and simultaneously we would be diversifying away from the preponderance of Time stock.

Once the cash from Betsy's former 401(k) was rolled into her IRA account, we would redirect it into several different mutual funds. Betsy's outlook was moderately cautious so we had 50 percent of her money in growth and income funds (specifically utility shares, REIT, and balanced funds), 25 percent in pure growth and global funds, 15 percent in emerging growth stock funds, and 10 percent in Treasuries.

Betsy's retirement looks pretty secure at this point largely due to her having contributed to a 401(k) from the beginning. Converting some of her income from taxable to tax-free will give her more on the bottom line. With her new approach to saving and paying herself a specific amount per month from her brokerage check writing account, it looks as if she is all clear for sailing or flying as often as she wants later on.

Claire, Single, Age 45
Short-term goal: pay off her mortgage
Medium-term goal: early retirement
Long-term goal: college education for her nephew

Claire's situation is quite similar to Betsy's except for her cash in-flow and her risk-tolerance. Claire is a self-employed photographer. She works mainly on annual reports for corporations. When the economy is good and businesses are willing to put a lot of artwork in their reports, she does well. When it is cost-cutting time, her costs are one of the first to go. She set up her own Keogh plan twelve years ago as a money-purchase plan. This way, in the high-earning years, she put away as much as she could to balance the off years. Her Keogh is now worth just over $125,000. Her financial caution worked in her favor in that in the years that she was flush and she had money left after contributing the maximum to her Keogh, she also put $2,000 in an IRA.

Claire loves the ocean and bought a home on Cape Cod at the high point of the eighties. She has refinanced the house but still has an outstanding mortgage of about $60,000. Other than the house, she has no outstanding debts. She owns a car and has never borrowed against her credit card. Claire is very cautious with her money. While Betsy knew what her salary would be per year (not including an annual bonus), Claire's earnings are unpredictable. And while Betsy was willing to invest more in the stock market, Claire was nervous about price fluctuations in her principal amount.

A more or less current rule of thumb says that in order to have a comfortable retirement, one will have to save three to four times her salary in addition to a pension and Social Security, to be able to live off the interest. If Claire took a good year as an example, say a year she made $90,000, she would have to have saved between $270,000 and $360,000 for retirement purposes. A year in which she made half that much would require significantly less savings to finance her retirement.

Claire has fifteen years to go to retirement if she keeps to her vow to be out of the work force by age sixty. If one projects from today's income and today's savings, she should be fine. However, a lot can change in fifteen years—including both her cash in-flow and inflation destroying that simple formula. Assuming also that she will enjoy a long life in retirement, her money's going to have to continue to work for her during her retirement years.

It seemed best to advise Claire to forgo the IRA contributions in favor of paying off her mortgage. She is able to claim as an expense part of her house and even her car for her business.

Those deductions add up to a lot more than the $2,000 IRA deduction. It was a hard thing to suggest, but Claire really needs to be more aggressive in promoting herself. If she wants to be able to meet all her financial goals successfully on the timetable she has set for herself, she has to make sure that her current cashflow remains steady.

It was one thing to prompt Claire into being more aggressive in her business approach. Her low risk-tolerance would not permit it in her investments. Her IRA is invested in zero coupon bonds scheduled to mature during the years she is sixty to sixty-five. Her Keogh consists of Treasury notes, certificates of deposit, and short-term bond funds. All the maturities are staggered, so she does benefit from changes in interest rates.

Claire's living needs are not extravagant. Unlike Betsy, she does not plan on traveling the world in her retirement. She simply wants to spend time in her mortgage-free house, learn and practice new art forms, and enjoy her nieces and nephews.

Claire's youngest sister has a one-year-old son to whom Claire is quite devoted. She wants to help him and her sister as much as possible. If she put as little as the equivalent of her previous IRA contributions into a custodian account for her nephew, and bought zero coupon Treasuries for him, he would be on his way to having a head start on his college tuition.

Sonya, 47, Divorced, No Children

Short-term goal: make money fast to finance an early retirement which she has neglected to prepare for

Sonya is a last brief example of a single woman client in her forties. To her credit, she is one of the many women now involved in an investment club. Unfortunately, she also gives witness to the truism that a little bit of knowledge is a dangerous thing. Sonya is a college professor but all of her out-of-class hours are now spent surfing between CNBC, the "Nightly Business Report," and CNN. She reads all the weekly money magazines and studies the *Wall Street Journal* and *Investor's Business Daily.* This plethora of material is confusing her. She is listening to too many opinions and she does not have the experience yet to sift between views.

She calls me more than once a week to ask if we should switch out of one mutual fund into another, or if we should move out of the airlines and into foods. She is trying to outguess market rotations. We may make one or more calls correctly, but this is a losing strategy over even the short term. She has forgotten her original investment plan as well as forgetting that investing has to be done with a longer view. If I were to move her funds as often as she calls, I myself would be accused of churning the account.

Sonya has to return to the basics of investing or she is going to lose all her money in this futile whipping around of her funds.

Elinor, Married, No Children, Age 49
Short-term goal: tax-advantaged saving
Medium-term goal: provide for parents
Long-term goal: divided year between Manhattan and Boca Raton

Elinor is an executive vice-president at a large manufacturing company. She has worked there ever since she received her MBA. She owns a great deal of company stock at this point. She has participated in the 401(k) for fifteen years. She is happy in her job and her title reflects her increased responsibilities and her annual salary of $110,000.

Elinor's husband, Rick, is a marketing manager for a national cosmetics company. He has a base pay which is augmented by receiving an override bonus on the business his division produces. His upside salary potential is unlimited. His company does not offer a 401(k) plan but he is vested in its pension and profit-sharing plan.

Their home in the Philadelphia suburbs is fully paid for.

They have IRAs set up in the years when the contributions were deductible. The IRAs still exist, but Elinor and Rick do not fund them anymore.

Every year Elinor calls me to run by me the choices of funds her firm offers for 401(k) investments. She is widely diversified with a distinct bent toward growth and international funds. In fact, she is a little too widely diversified. Her company seems to provide as wide a choice of funds as it can, and each year Elinor likes to go with the newest. Yet she keeps every fund she has ever picked from the preceding years instead of switching some of her past investments into the newer choices.

Six or seven different funds are sufficient. I am not saying you always have to stick with your original choices, but if Elinor wants to add a new fund from time to time, it would be better if she moved out of another one at the same time. Equally, it would not make sense to put all of your money in only one or two funds. It is as counterproductive to be under-diversified as it is to be over.

Elinor and Rick have a JTWROS brokerage account (see page 116) with me. We have bought some quality growth stocks. The other half of their portfolio is invested in Pennsylvania tax-free bonds. In order to meet Elinor's short- and medium-term goals, I suggested she buy a variable annuity. She'd accomplish three things:

1. More of her money would be working for her on a tax-deferred basis.
2. She could name her parents beneficiaries of the annuity should something happen to her.
3. She could continue in her preference for growth investments by means of a variable, rather than fixed, annuity.

Elinor and Rick should have no problem meeting all of their goals, assuming their professional lives continue as they have up until now. Their long-term goal can be met by selling their home (another of their growth assets) when they are ready to relocate. They will benefit from the one-time $125,000 exclusion. This exclusion means they will receive this one-of-a-kind and once-in-a-lifetime tax break. If you sell your home after you are age fifty-five or older, you are allowed to keep up to $125,000 of the profit completely tax-free.

Justine, Married, Age 53
One goal: retirement

Justine came to see me on her cousin's recommendation about two years ago. Justine works for a private health-care provider and her salary is $80,000. She is covered under a SEP plan at work, has excellent medical coverage, and doesn't want to contribute to an IRA because her contribution is not a deduction.

She has a grown son from her first marriage and her second husband has no dependents. Her husband Hugh is a high school principal. His retirement needs are being met by his TIAA/CREF contributions. During his summer vacations, he sometimes gives lectures and has written articles for scholarly magazines.

Hugh was eligible to open a Keogh account because of his outside income. He and his accountant decided on a money-purchase plan and he has just begun to fund this Keogh with high-dividend-paying stocks and some balanced mutual funds.

Justine is almost obsessive in her focus on retirement, but I truly do not think I can give her any assurance. The problem is that she has only one small personal account and she does not appear to be able to save. She calls me and asks what is the minimum she can add to her account. I tell her she can put in whatever she wants whenever she wants. She says I can expect money soon, but it never comes.

Her personal account is invested 25 percent in zero coupon bonds, for a protective cushion, and 75 percent in quality growth stocks. Her account grew 14 percent last year, which was a stellar market year anyway. No matter how well I perform, however, I can't increase her principal a thousandfold. If she cannot help herself by making herself save, I am not able to help her that much either. The older a woman gets, the greater the percentage of her earnings she has to force herself to put aside for retirement.

Amelia, Married, Two Children, Age 48
Lisa, Married, Two Children, Age 47
Short- and medium-term goal: college tuition
Long-term goal: retirement

I am using Amelia and Lisa as contrasting stories. Amelia's older daughter will be ready for college in six years. Her younger has ten years to go. Amelia opened a custodian account for each child before their first birthday. She regularly contributes to these accounts and has asked her in-laws to do the same for her girls' celebratory occasions. We have consistently bought zero coupon bonds over the years. Her older daughter is too old now to make a zero investment that can double the invested amount so, since the time frame is shorter, we have expanded into some income and growth mutual funds. Funds are higher risk than the zero coupon bonds in general, but an equity income fund is a conservative choice. Some growth is justified in her account by now. All dividends and capital gains are reinvested, and our planning seems to be on target.

Amelia and Joe's retirement needs have taken a back seat to their girls' education needs. Amelia's a chef. She has an IRA that she contributes $2,000 to each year. Her job can be a well-paid one, but the nature of the job is not one that allows her to take advantage of any in-house retirement plans. She has consciously postponed saving for her own retirement until she knows college tuitions are set.

Lisa's attitude is the reverse. "I'm not putting my retirement at risk to get my kids through college," she said to me a few years back. "They're in private schools now, but that's as far as I go."

Lisa and her husband are architects and work for themselves. They are renting a home now but spend their free time designing the dream house they want for retirement. They both have Keogh and IRA plans. Lisa's investments tend to be more aggressive; her husband is moderately cautious.

Lisa does not consider herself selfish; she says she is just being realistic. She lives in a town where her children can attend good state colleges. Her goal is not that her children go to Ivy League schools where the tuition is climbing to over $30,000 a year. A public college or a university in another state is completely acceptable to her.

Sarah, Divorced, Three Children, Age 51
Short-term goal: find a new job
Medium-term goal: buy a house
Long-term goal: retirement

Sarah's divorce has just become final. Her children are ten, thirteen, and sixteen. The only thing she feels good about regarding the long divorce proceedings is that she has her ex-husband paying for college education for all three children—and, unlike Lisa, she stipulated that no school be excluded because of its tuition rates. For this benefit, however, she gave up receiving any other child support as well as a portion of her husband's pension plan. Her former husband insisted that any other payments to her would be in the form of alimony so that he could get the tax deduction.

Sarah needs a job to help pay for living expenses as well as to help her in her own retirement goals. She knows she will be better about saving if she can have automatic deductions taken from her paycheck.

She had been making small contributions to her children's custodian accounts in the past. There was no necessity for her to continue this now because their educational funding was provided for. It became much more important for her to put money away to help herself in her own future needs.

Sarah lives in Massachusetts, a high tax state. She is not going to be able to claim her children as dependents, so it seems advisable to put her personal savings into a tax-free Massachusetts bond mutual fund. Again, to take temptation out of the way, Sarah chose to reinvest both dividends and capital gains.

Sarah's first inclination when we spoke about investments was not an unusual one. Any woman who has lost the lifestyle she used to have is eager to re-create it as soon as possible. The way to do that is not by increasing risk, though, but by systematic planning. Sarah originally told me she wanted to buy the most aggressive mutual fund, instead of a tax-free one, to make a killing. She was going for the whole nine yards, the promise of the highest return, instead of one foot at a time. Her own financial situation was entirely too vulnerable to defend this kind of move. In the best of times, aggressive purchases should not make up more than about one quarter of the most adventurous portfolio— and they must be looked at as longer-term holdings.

Sarah's medium-term goal of wanting her own house won't be a realistic one until she finds a job and is able to save from her salary and build up her own net worth. It is equally difficult here to predict how best she can prepare for retirement. Again, participating in a retirement plan at work will start her on the way. If she is able to meet her medium-term goal, the house itself will become an asset to use for retirement planning.

Melanie, Widowed, Age 55
Short-term goal: understand her finances
Medium-term goal: sell her house; move in-state or out

Melanie's husband died suddenly in his sleep less than a year ago. He had always taken care of all the family finances. He had tried to include Melanie, but she simply was not interested and thought he would always be there.

His records were complete. His estate was settled easily and quickly but the lawyer and accountant themselves were not able to get Melanie involved.

Now she was ready at least to talk about things. We looked at the portfolio she had inherited. Many of the stocks and bonds should remain as they were. Her husband had owned AT&T stock for over twenty-five years and had kept all of the subsequent offshoots. There was a tremendous capital gain on his original purchase price but Melanie's new cost basis became the price of the stocks on the day her husband died. We decided to keep all these communication stocks.

There were some of what we in the business call dogs, however. Her husband had taken a few flyers which had not panned out. Melanie felt out of loyalty she should not sell anything her husband had bought.

"It'll work out," she insisted to me.

"Did he always keep everything he bought?" I asked.

"Oh, no. I didn't listen that much but he was always talking about his trading stocks. If they disappointed him, he was off on another kick."

I explained to Melanie that these few laggards were his trading stocks and that the telephone stocks were what are called investment stocks. Since for these stocks too, she would have a different cost basis, she should sell them and her own loss would not be as great as his would have been.

Melanie was awarded half of the private pension her husband had accumulated at his corporate job. She was not able to make an investment decision for that money now, so we put it in a six-month Treasury bill as a resting place.

I suggested Melanie may want to take a course specifically directed toward women in her local college's adult education program. She would see she was not alone in her need for knowledge and she would be able to build up some confidence in her own ability to be responsible for her inheritance. I did not want Melanie to fall into the money-paralysis syndrome. Many women when widowed or left an inheritance from parents are afraid to move this money around. They leave it in low-risk investments. This kind of total nondiversification will not even keep pace with inflation over time.

It was also too soon for Melanie to decide about where she wanted to live. The house was too big for her but it was the only place she knew. The mortgage was paid up and there was no rush for her to move out.

Her first priority was to reexamine the careful paper trail her husband had always left and to try to learn from it. Melanie needed to get some financial experience of her own before she could make other life decisions.

As we've seen, these fifteen years can cover a wide spectrum of life events. The main goals which predominate for this cycle are:

- prepare for education funding needs
- pay heightened attention to retirement monies
- reevaluate need for tax-advantaged opportunities
- increase your own personal net worth
- make provision for elderly parents if necessary
- examine single-name versus joint-name property holdings.

Overall, the most important goal during this period is to guarantee for yourself as best you can that you will have the money you need when you need it.

17

Ages Fifty-Five and Up

MOST OF THIS AGE SPAN will cover our retirement years. But let us think optimistically and plan for it to last much longer than the fifteen years allotted to the previous two age spans. After all, even the most ruthless IRS calculations use an age expectancy of eighty-six when mandating certain minimum withdrawals from retirement plans after age 70½.

There are still investment strategies to be followed and utilized during these years. No matter what your risk-tolerance, part of the retirement years goals will be living as well as you can off your money as well as leaving what you intend to your beneficiaries. A conservative approach is to maintain safety of your principal amount while drawing a regular income, either taxable or tax-free, from it. A less conservative path is to aim for building more wealth and see a growth of that principal.

There are important tax consequences to consider during this period. You will want to be aware how much of your Social Security payments are being taxed. What are the tax implications when you begin annuitizing or withdrawing from any of your long-established retirement plans? Who in fact should be named as beneficiary for each plan in order to maximize your own income while at the same time protect this money for your heirs?

You might be the recipient from any number of retirement programs all at once. For most women, distributions any time after age 59½ are the single largest amount of money they will have accumulated over their lifetimes. How do you deal with this lump sum of money?

Your state of residence might play an important part in your tax planning. This is also a good time to review your will and to revisit the issue of creating trusts. Review whose assets are held in whose name and make sure your choice of beneficiaries is up-to-date.

At this age, you still might be responsible for the care of your parents in addition to facing medical needs of your own. Single, nonworking women may find this stage particularly frightening if they have no health coverage from a spouse or previous employer.

Investing doesn't stop with this cycle. It starts all over again, often with entirely new objectives. Your money life is entering a new cycle as well. Whether you (or your husband)have opted for early retirement in order to spend quality time together, whether you are single and still working, or whether you are newly divorced or widowed, these years are probably going to see you set a new life direction.

Setting goals at this stage will have more immediacy. Specifying short-, medium-, and long-term goals may not be realistic because of the shortened span of years between them. It makes sense for goals and their time periods to overlap. Nevertheless, it is still worth it to sit down and reexamine your finances with the help of the worksheets in the beginning of this book.

You may be entering a whole new quarter of your life. This is a period of time with all new challenges—challenges that are financial, physical, and emotional. Make these years be your golden years in the true meaning of that word. You have met the responsibilities and obligations of the other two age spans. This is the time to really enjoy what you have accomplished and give yourself the opportunity to appreciate each day. As an eighty-two-year-old widowed client who had been through a series of rough years said to me the other day, "I'm doing just wonderfully. I get up and run every day!" She meant that figuratively, not literally, but I could hear the contentment in her voice.

There are four main issues to address in these years:

- estate planning
- home equity and ownership
- providing for elderly parents (or younger children)
- withdrawals from retirement plans

Estate Planning

An important part of estate planning is getting the right tax adviser. I am familiar with the types of trusts that are available and what they can do, but only your own lawyer or accountant will know what will work best for you and your own family setup. What I do is money management. You will need that once certain types of trusts are created. First, take the time to get the kind of tax advice you need. Have that professional review your will in light of current estate-tax rules. That professional will suggest to you the exact mechanisms to keep as much of the wealth you have built out of Uncle Sam's, trustees', and even some executors' hands.

I am not on the trust bandwagon per se, but I can assure you from my own experience that a couple of the benefits of setting up a *living trust* outweigh any of the cost or time incurred. A living trust means just that—you set up the trust while you are still alive. The trust can be tailored to accomplish your own precise goals. That again is for you and your tax adviser to deal with.

When you open a living trust, you arrange to have the assets within that trust given to your heirs without having to rely on a will and without having to go through probate. That is benefit number one. Probate is costly—especially if you live in California, New York, or Florida—and is time-consuming.

And probate is public. That is reason number two. Wills are public documents. Trusts are not (unless they are created by the will). A living trust keeps quiet about what you have while you are alive and maintains that silence about your affairs when you die.

Your House

Many women fund a great deal of their retirement through their home. I do not mean by taking in boarders. Your residence, particularly if you have lived in it a long time and the mortgage is paid up, may represent a substantial personal asset.

Real estate values fluctate just as equities do, but they are presumably more stable than tangibles or fine arts. Overall, housing is regarded as an appreciating asset.

Earlier I discussed the tax preference for selling a home after the age of fifty-five. Let me review some of the details.

Rose, the newly exuberant widow I just mentioned, lived in the same house for almost fifty years. She and her husband had raised three children in that house. Even when their children were long gone, she and Roy did not want to sell the house. They needed all the rooms for holiday visits. Rose still could not bear to sell the house when Roy died. She did the proverbial rattling around the rooms, the roof needed repairs, the real estate taxes escalated, and her vow not to touch her principal was eroding under these pressures.

Her middle daughter is an accountant and finally got her to see the wisdom in selling the house and buying a condominium in a nearby senior citizens retirement park.

The house sold for $250,000. It had originally been bought for $40,000, so the entire gain was $210,000. Rose did not have to declare the first $125,000 of the gain because she had, obviously, lived in the home for three of the five years preceding the sale and was over age 55. The new apartment cost $150,000.

Another aspect of this tax law states that if you reinvest the balance of the sales price *in excess of $125,000* in another residence, you will not have to recognize that gain either until this new residence is sold. Rose had $85,000 in gains after the first exclusion. She could use $25,000 against this $85,000 by her condo purchase. She would only have capital gains tax left to pay on $60,000.

The sale and consecutive buy also meant that Rose had

$100,000 in cash to invest that she did not have before. After segregating the amount we figured she would need to cover six months' living expenses, we had money to add back to her principal to create a heightened cashflow for her. No wonder she is out "running."

Elderly or Dependent Parents

The so-called sandwich years may not end with the middle cycle of years where at least it can be assumed you are still earning a paycheck. In retirement you may be faced with the puzzle of figuring out how to ensure the cashflow to meet your own needs for twenty to thirty years, while at the same time facing the financial responsibilities of aged parents or still dependent children.

Two of the methods are the same for either the younger or older generation—that is, without worrying where the money is going to come from! As mentioned earlier, you may set up a custodial account in which you are the custodian for another person. That account is designated for IRS purposes by the other person's Social Security number and is taxed at the other person's lower income tax rate.

Second, you may open a joint account with either a parent or a child. The Social Security number may be either yours or the other person's, depending upon who will be recognized the owner for tax purposes. The point of the joint account is for those assets to go, without probate again, to the co-owner at either owner's death.

A third option, more for medical or emergency decisions, is to have your parent(s) give you a power of attorney so that you can make any decisions which may be necessary for them if they are incapable of making those decisions for themselves for any reason.

Withdrawing From Retirement Accounts

No one ever said the IRS was fair. In the case of taking money out of your IRA (the rules are the same for Keoghs and 401[k]s), you are damned if you withdraw too much when you are under 59½ and similarly damned if you withdraw too little after age 70½. First you cannot take it, and then you must take it—and the penalties for not taking it are much more severe than dipping into the pot too soon.

There are exceptions: you can start withdrawing before age 59½ if you use IRS formulas to schedule equal distributions at regular intervals for the rest of your life with some modifications. For the purpose of this book, however, I would prefer to focus on the majority of retirees. In general, over and above the withdrawal amount counting as income, the withdrawal will be subject to a 10 percent penalty if you take it out of your plan prior to age 59½.

You can basically do no wrong in the years between ages 59½ and 70½. You may withdraw in an *unrestricted* manner, withdrawing as often or as much as you like. (Should you take out more than $150,000 in any one year, with some exceptions, you may be liable for a 15 percent penalty.)

You may receive regularly scheduled or single sum payments as you request them. You may receive the payments in cash or in securities. No matter what your age, these payments will be taxed as ordinary income. (Again, there is an exception. If you made nondeductible contributions to an IRA in 1987 or after, a portion of each withdrawal will be exempt from taxation because you made the contribution with after-tax money.)

The custodian of your retirement plan will usually give you a choice of automatic withholding of federal and state income taxes.

Sophie's unconcerned withdrawal years are coming to a close. She is going to be 70½ on January 26, 1997. What this means for her and the IRS is that she *must* begin receiving distributions of the specified minimum amount no later than April 1, 1998. For the first year, there is a three-month grace period. Sophie may begin her required distributions any time during 1997, or she may defer the first withdrawal until April 1, l998. If she defers, she will be liable for another distribution that same year no later than December 31. In all subsequent years, she must take an annual required amount prior to December 31.

The IRS can end up having the last laugh on you if you do not wise up by that key April 1 date. After you turn 70½, you have to make some choices by April 1 that are irrevocable. These choices relate to your beneficiary and also to your choice of a fixed or a recalculated life expectancy.

Let us talk about your heirs. If you are married, most commonly you will leave your retirement plan to your husband. At your death, your husband then has the option of putting this account in his own name and starting over with new heirs.

Sophie and Max had talked this out together. Each named the other as beneficiary. Their further objective was that the surviving spouse would in turn claim it as his or her own and in turn name their son Raymond as new heir. In the haste to get your affairs in order after a death, do remember that the new owner name and heir will be eligible for the stretched-out or extended payout period only if all this is arranged for *before* withdrawing any money.

Naming Raymond was done out of planning needs, but Sophie and Max were far from thinking about their demise. They are both fitness advocates and intended to use their savings and their withdrawals to finance the trekking, skiing, and biking trips they look forward to taking. They live in Florida in a mortgage-free house. They have no reason to sell this house. Because Florida has no state tax, they can buy municipal bonds from any state without worrying about taxes at the state level. I structured a portfolio for them of staggered maturities ranging over a span of ten years to take advantage of all ebbs and flows of the interest-rate cycle.

When a growth stock had reached its potential in Sophie's individual account, we switched the proceeds into investment tools that threw off more income, like utility stocks and REITs. Sophie and Max were in a lower income tax bracket during retirement than they were earlier, and the taxable income would

.lter that bracket. As an added protection for Raymond, Sophie switched her brokerage account to be a JTWROS with her son.

Maude faced an entirely different scenario. Her company terminated its own retirement plan when she was fifty-six. Maude, while still an employee, became responsible for her own retirement planning. She did not elect the early retirement option offered to her because she wanted to continue working until mandatory retirement age, which was sixty-eight. She is now seventy and must withdraw. Previously she rolled the lump sum she received when the corporate plan terminated into a brokerage house IRA account. She also began to participate in the newly inaugurated 401(k) plan.

Since at that time she was making a salary that was more than enough to meet her immediate needs, she felt she could concentrate on more growth-oriented investments than normally one would at her age. In her rollover IRA, she and I had gradually developed a portfolio of growth stocks with diversification in mind. We had also put 20 percent of her portfolio in zero coupon bonds scheduled to mature when she was seventy. That way, if we did not want to sell or transfer out a stock to meet her minimum distribution requirements, we would have cash on hand from the zeros to meet the requirement instead.

Maude decided to be a bit more conservative with the 401(k) money, since she was not as familiar with the fund managers. She split her money between three equity income funds. By the time she retired, she had over $300,000 in total retirement funds. Because her estate was a sizeable one, Maude had to be as careful with the withdrawal amounts from her IRA as she was with the rest of her money.

The withdrawals were taxable income but that did not mean that she needed to redeploy them in more taxable vehicles. I suggested that we automatically buy short-term tax-free bonds of Illinois, her place of residence, each time she took the withdrawal. At least she would save herself a form of double taxation at the same time that she would be receiving some form of tax-free cashflow.

As a single woman with no extended family she cared to support, she first put her estate as her beneficiary. She had named several charities in her will and assumed that that was the best way to dispose of her retirement funds as well.

The IRS will get your money this way, too. If your heir is your estate or a revocable trust, your retirement plan proceeds become taxable at your death. Since Maude did not want to name a person as heir, I suggested she name one or more of the particular tax-exempt charities as direct heirs of her IRA. A charity will inherit the entire amount free from income tax plus the estate gets a deduction against estate tax.

The other irrevocable choice is how to determine your life expectancy. One aspect of the choice depends on whether or not you are using a joint or single life expectancy. The second choice is which method you are going to use for the calculation. You are not allowed to change the method of calculation once you have chosen.

Devising a payment schedule essentially involves dividing the worth of your account by your life expectancy. The hook is who you name as a beneficiary and if that beneficiary is your spouse or not. When you designate a beneficiary, you are allowed to average out your two life expectancies. If the beneficiary is not your husband, however, you can only use a maximum ten-year differential. In other words, the IRS is intent on making you take out as much as possible sooner rather than later, because it's getting a piece of the action.

If you recall, the penalty for withdrawing too much when you are under 59½ was a bearable 10 percent. No such luck for withdrawing too little after you are 70½. You'll pay a hefty 50 percent penalty for your inattention.

All life expectancies are determined using the tables included in the regulations published by the IRS. A single life expectancy is self-explanatory. A joint may be used between you and your husband or between you and a nonspouse.

The tables use the age you will be on your birthday in the year you turn 70½. Sophie will be 70½ in January 1997. Since she will be 71 in July 1997, she will use age 71 to determine the life-expectancy factor for the withdrawal she must take no later than April 1, l998. Then she'll use seventy-two for the subsequent withdrawal to take place by December 31 of that same year, and so forth.

Some women who are married still are able to choose the single life expectancy factor. Even though a joint life-expectancy factor will always result in a lower required distribution amount, a woman may want to receive a larger amount as her minimum.

Hortense curtailed her spending until her seventieth birthday. Even though she wanted more income, she wanted even more for her IRA to accrue interest tax-deferred as long as possible. Her husband was already withdrawing from his retirement plan using both their ages for his joint life-expectancy factor. Hortense, though she could have done the same, elected to receive her required minimum distributions using the single factor.

Lastly, what method are you going to use for calculating your life expectancy? None of this is guesswork. The tables are set by the Internal Revenue Service. The most common method of figuring your distribution amount is the *recalculation* method. This method refigures your life expectancy every year.

When Sophie will be 71, her husband Max will be 68. Under joint life-expectancy tables, the life expectancy is 21.2 years. Imagine she had $150,000 in her retirement plan. That amount divided by 21.2 means she will have to withdraw a minimum of $7,075 that year. The following year she will have to recalculate returning to the life-expectancy table she originally used to calculate her first distribution.

The alternate method, referred to as *term certain*, means that you make withdrawals over a fixed term calculated just once—when you are 70½. Many women do not choose this method because they worry about outliving their IRA. There has got to be some reason to pick this method, though, right? There is an estate-planning benefit to picking this method. When either you or your beneficiary die, the distributions continue over the same number of years as was originally determined, as opposed to the recalculation method when the life expectancy factor will change at date of death.

Without overstating this, I must reiterate that whichever method you choose for determining life expectancy, you cannot change your mind under any circumstance.

What you can change your mind about is anything you do with that money before and after age 70½. Again, we'll look at a few women and what choices they made.

Edith, Divorced, Grown Children, Age 57
Short-/medium-term goal: save more aggressively for the next 13 years
Longer-term goal: take adult education classes; travel

Edith's child support payments have ceased since her two children are both over twenty-one. She receives $10,000 alimony, taxable to her, a year. As part of the divorce settlement, she received half of her husband's IRA, which amounted to $50,000 at the time. That account has grown to close to $100,000 but is only about half of what she would like to have accumulated by her seventieth birthday.

She's employed as a bookkeeper for a furniture designer and is covered by this small firm's SEP. She owns a small house in Connecticut and takes the train into New York for work. By living out of state, she saves both New York State and City taxes.

There isn't a great deal Edith can do to augment her situation, especially since she is risk-averse. I suggested she contribute further to the IRA even though she would not be able to deduct the contributions. The tax-deferred compounding of her money would be more beneficial for her than leaving it in a personal account, and we could aim for the highest, yet safest, income return.

Edith admitted to me that her son came around sometimes

looking for some handouts. She was generous by nature but now was worried about what she needed to accomplish financially for herself over the next decade. Putting money into an IRA would automatically make those monies unavailable to her grown children.

Edith was eligible for the $125,000 exclusion on a house sale because the house she and her husband had lived in was in his name and was sold that way. Her house was worth at least the amount of the exclusion. She might want to think about selling it in a few years, using those proceeds to finance her retirement further and rent an apartment closer to wherever she wanted to pursue her studies.

She had done some inquiries in her neighborhood and learned that she might be able to pick up some more work on weekends, especially around year-end and income tax time. Depending upon how much money she made, she might decide to establish a Keogh plan for herself. She also may be able to deduct part of her house as a home office. At the very least she would be increasing her take-home pay and could invest that money for her future needs. Until she made a decision about selling the house, she needed to concentrate on making and saving money, not spending it or giving it away.

Sylvia, Widowed, Age 81

Goals: meet her living needs; try not to go into her principal; help her children and grandchildren on occasion; stay independent

Sylvia continues to live in the two-story home she shared with her husband and family, but she has made two houses out of the one. She lives on the ground floor and she rents out the top floor. She has been doing this for several years and the rent she receives has more than paid her back for the reconstruction necessary to create two living spaces. The rent also helps her cashflow and both she and her children feel better knowing she has someone on her premises should she need anything.

Sylvia's husband was a doctor and was the owner of a large

tax-deferred annuity. Half of this was left to her in his will and the other half to their four children. Sylvia takes monthly withdrawals and has chosen to do so at a fixed amount based on life-expectancy tables used by the insurance company.

Sylvia also has a long-running personal brokerage account. She started this account when her children were grown with money she saved from her and her husband's checking account. She first started buying certificates of deposit at her bank but when interest rates fell, and she had over $50,000 set aside, she decided to learn what other options were available to her.

She never touched her investment money while her husband was still alive. He practiced until the day he died from a massive heart attack, and his income comfortably covered their living expenses, vacations, and occasional temporary loans to their children.

Sylvia inherited stocks and bonds from her husband valued at close to $300,000. He had held many of the stocks for over thirty years—blue chips that he had been traditionally told to buy and put away and forget. This advice had worked for him. He owned IBM, General Motors, Gillette, and all the telephone stocks. They had split several times and the price he had originally paid was miniscule compared to current value.

I explained to Sylvia about the stepped-up cost basis. She should not sell any of the stocks while they were held in estate name because the estate would have to pay a huge capital gains tax. She should wait until the stocks were reregistered in her own name. With her new cost basis reflecting current stock prices (calculated either using date of death or six months later price) later, she could sell if we decided to and her capital gain tax would not be prohibitive.

We did sell some of the growth stocks and reinvested the proceeds into higher-yielding securities. Sylvia still had not wanted to touch the principal even after he died, but that was unrealistic. I told her that her husband had left her this money so that she could continue in the same lifestyle that they had had together. There was no need for her to cut back. They had made this money and it was hers to enjoy and use as she saw fit now.

Sylvia decided to take a fixed monthly amount from her brokerage account in the same way in which she was received the annuity. We started with $1,000 a month and agreed that we would see how that worked out. If she needed to increase it over time, we would. Unless interest rates dropped precipitously, we would not be going into her principal even with this allowance. Nevertheless, we agreed always to keep $10,000 in the money market, so that if she needed an extra check for taxes, house repairs, or for any other unforeseen event, the cash would always be available.

Sylvia's financial knowledge has grown over the years, but especially so since she was widowed. More than once she has said to me that she wished she had paid attention earlier. She was content to have her husband manage all their money. I reminded her that that was not completely so because she had started investing for herself all on her own. Still she said, in hindsight, if she could do it all over, she would have saved from the very beginning. She liked making money decisions for herself and knowing that she was building some wealth of her own even at this age.

Sylvia was lucky in that her husband did provide well for her. Other women may not have that luxury. It is never too late to learn, but the earlier the better if you want to control your own financial destiny.

Several of my elderly women clients elect the same type of monthly payout that Sylvia did. A monthly allowance is steadier than simply taking out the interest or dividends that accrue each month. The reliability of the monthly checks gives the security of knowing you can pay your monthly bills, because it is predicated on that need. It is best to keep this type of investment money in low-risk, shorter-term investments (Treasuries, two-year corporate or tax-free bonds, income stocks) to prevent both inflation outpacing income and the principal amount being vulnerable to a loss should an investment have to be liquidated.

There are some basic rules for investment during this age span. Some of the rules apply to any age, but they are worth paying special attention to during your retirement years:

1. Keep good records.

Sylvia's husband kept a record of the purchase price of every stock he bought. He is the exception. In my twenty years in the business, I find that women generally keep better records than men. Many of my women clients know when their dividends will arrive, know what the equity is in their account, and record all stock splits. Somehow this expertise has not gotten passed down to their children and grandchildren.

Do not let that happen to you. Good record keeping is invaluable—not only for you during your lifetime, but for your heirs when they have to dispose of your estate according to your instructions.

2. Think about creating trusts for your grandchildren.

If you want to put something away for grandchildren to help with their college education or whatever, think about setting up a small trust for them instead of the custodian account. The trusts do not expire at age eighteen the way a custodian account does, and the principal does not automatically go to the beneficiary at that age. A trust has its own tax identification number and is taxed at a preferential rate. You can continue to fund the trust as long as you like and it will not go to the beneficiary until your death.

3. Don't ignore growth.

Financial needs during retirement will necessitate some portfolio readjustment, but do not totally ignore growth. Bonds provide reliable income, but inflation can affect the purchasing power of that income. Keep bonds short term with staggered maturities. If possible, aim to keep about 20 percent of your portfolio in growth-oriented investments.

4. Do not forget about diversification.

No matter how little or how great your investment slice is during retirement years, you can still create some diversification. Loading up on only one stock, one bond, or even one certificate of deposit is not sensible. You can receive the same predictable income by including some variety in your portfolio.

5. Beware of a tax-avoidance obsession

Fear of Uncle Sam can lead you into thinking you need more tax-free income than you truly do. If you pass a certain break-point in your tax-free income, you may be subject to the alternative minimum tax. Pay attention to your tax bracket and talk to your tax adviser. You may find that you can do better—even after paying the IRS—on some taxable investments.

In sum, there are five important sources of income at retirement:

- Social Security
- company-sponsored retirement plans
- self-employed retirement plans
- your IRA
- your own personal savings and investment

None of these five alone is likely to provide for all of your retirement income needs. The more of them that you have been able to utilize—and the sooner you began planning—the better equipped you will be to withstand inflation, market and interest rate fluctuations, and any upcoming changes in the tax code.

PART V: HOW

18

What to Read and Watch

THE "HOW" PART of building personal wealth will help you in your everyday approach to investing. The chapter on reading and watching will give you suggestions for each, depending upon your level of interest and financial sophistication. Before you oversubscribe in a flurry of enthusiasm, try to realistically assess the amount of extracurricular time you really can devote to media homework.

The next two chapters on investing do's and investing don'ts will give you rules that should be followed in any kind of economy. Moreover, by paying attention to these rules, you will be learning the ropes of how to ride out either jolting or boring stock market times. Sometimes you have to make sure your head is in order before you can correctly order your finances.

If this were a book on nutrition, I would be reminding you that you are what you eat. Put into financial language, I say that your investments are a by-product of what you read and what you hear.

Even if women are incorrectly characterized by not being able to talk about money adequately, they certainly are thinking about it. They probably are listening to a great deal of money talk as well.

The *Nightly Business Report* conducted a recent survey. Both men and women were asked what their main source of information about money and investing was. The number one source for

147

both groups were newspapers and magazines, and the percentages were not totally dissimilar. Of the men, 55 percent chose this answer compared to 49.9 percent for the women.

Interestingly enough, investment clubs were the women's second highest-rated source (26.1 percent) versus only 2.8 percent for men, evidence of women's comfort in group situations.

For both groups, online services, television/radio, and broker/financial adviser all outranked the friends/family category. The media sources were not taken as gospel. Over 60 percent of men and women said they considered the information but did more research on their own before acting. These numbers prove that there are plenty of people listening and reacting, especially since a mere 3 percent of those quizzed said the financial information was not useful.

Remember Sonya from chapter 16—the woman who was overresponding to everything she read? Sonya indisputably was reading the right names and quoting the right sources. She was, however, using these materials in a counterproductive way. She would look at the percentage gainers in the newspapers and think she had better buy before it was too late. She would fearfully scan the percentage loser column praying none of her stocks would be in that list.

She would hear a weather report for below-normal temperatures and wonder if she should buy grain stocks. Or she would hear a commodity report on rising natural gas prices and wonder if she should buy some futures—or if the futures were up to limit, should she go short instead?

She could not remember if George Soros liked gold this week or not. Was the Magellan Fund buying or selling technology stocks? Would the Fed really lower rates at its next meeting or would rates stay unchanged?

There is no question that each one of these elements affects the market daily, but trying to fashion your portfolio in tandem with any of these statements is not only an impossibility, it is often a situation of getting the news after the event itself has taken place.

If most of the above is gibberish to you, do not worry. Some of it is, some of it is also idle lunch-hour conversation, and all of it is rather esoteric taken on its own. Each statement does not really have a lot of meaning out of context. Market information does become influential over time if you begin to hear the same facts from different places and you see a distinct market pattern develop.

Every writer, be it for a radio script, a newspaper column, or a magazine article is going to have a bias. And each commentator is going to put his or her own spin on translating an economic event for the public. I do the same when I am talking to my own clients. My clients are asking me what I think about something. I will give my own opinion based on what I too have read, heard, and experienced. I try to put my thoughts and beliefs in the language I think my clients will understand. That is no different from any other media person. What I will try to do that is different, though, is refer to one of the more public opinions and say why I agree or disagree with the research for that particular client.

Analysts use two different data bases in trying to forecast market movement: *technical* and *fundamental.*

When you see any analyst on television using a graph or a chart, you know he or she is an advocate of technical analysis. A technician looks at daily volume figures, price-volume relationships, underlying patterns of supply and demand within the market itself, and various other statistics in order to determine the support (low) and resistance (high) level of any individual security. Buy or sell recommendations are made on the compilation of all this number gathering.

On CNBC, for example, when someone is commenting from a technical viewpoint, he or she is introduced precisely that way—as a technical analyst.

The majority of the market reporting that you will read about or hear on television carries a fundamental approach. The fundamental analyst looks at management, at earnings per share, and at the anticipated sales, profits, and expenditures of a particular company. These figures are put into context against whatever industry group is as a whole and current economic trends and, again, buy or sell recommendations are made.

There is no right or wrong in either one of these paths. It is a matter of preference and interest and, generally speaking, it is worth asking your broker what her firm's technical and fundamental recommendation is regarding a new purchase.

More important in your ongoing life is deciding what to read and what to listen to in terms of financial news and its impact on your own investment goals. And then, if you do manage to read the right columns or catch the appropriate and accurate business television news, how do you know how to interpret this news as an investor?

Let me examine two major topics of economic news and forecasts and see how they relate to you as an investor and a consumer. These topics are interest rates and oil prices.

In the early 80s, when the prime rate was close to 20 percent and money market funds yielded between 17 and 18 percent, anyone could afford to be a lazy investor. Not too many financial decisions are necessary when you are assured your money is going to compound at those lofty levels. In your wealth-building program, low-risk and cash investments at that time would be all you needed.

But what was good for the investor was not good for the economy. What if in your professional life you were a banker, a builder, a factory owner, or a real estate broker? Your business was drying up because people could not afford to take out loans. Houses were not being built or sold because construction loans and mortgage rates were too prohibitive. Plants could not expand and equipment was too expensive for which to borrow money.

On the one hand, it was comforting, and easy, to see your savings give you such a high rate of return. Yet you might have had to delve into these same savings more than you wanted in order to survive economically from your own business woes. Inflation was high and the U.S. economy was stalemated.

The cycle continues and you start to hear on the financial nightly news that the prime rate was lowered half a percentage point. A more detailed report may tell you that the federal funds rate went down a fraction. This is not a time to moan and groan because your money market yield is going down commensurably. As interest rates decline, business itself accelerates. True, the days of passive investing are over. Growth opportunities should be looked at as alternatives to pure income choices. It is time to shift your investments over time as the interest-rate climate shifts.

The price of oil has many ramifications as well. When prices are high, oil companies themselves make money. So do oil drilling and oil service companies. Oil rig and oil barge companies make good stock buys. At the same time, transportation issues take it on the chin.

When the pendulum swings the other way and lower oil prices prevail, automobiles begin to sell, plane fares are cheaper, and gas station owners are happier. People drive and fly more and more gasoline gets sold. Motel and hotel owners, resorts, and entertainment centers do more business because families can afford to get to them.

We all tend to personalize whatever news we hear on any topic. Money news is complicated because while on a self-interested level, we might prefer one scenario, that same scenario may not be desirable for the economy or the country as a whole.

Economics, interest rates, and inflation all concern a balancing of personal and industrial needs and with domestic and international relationships. The same way you listen to your local news within a framework of the national news, think of looking at your investment portfolio within the context of the national economy.

There are a myriad of sources of stock market information. My day starts with watching CNBC from the moment I get up until I leave for the office. If I am home for any reason during the day, I reflexively turn the television back on to that station. I also watch the *Nightly Business Report* while I do my stretching exercises every evening. I have watched some of these commentators for so many years that I feel as if we are all family.

This viewing is in addition to all my required reading. But the market is my job. What I have to do and what I like to do is not what you may choose to do. There are sources of informaton for every level of interest. The only area that lacks market information, I find, is the radio. As far as I know, there is only one national program devoted to business issues and that program, "Marketplace," is on NPR weekday evenings.

I would also say that the two sentences on the local or national news simply announcing what the stockmarket did for the day and the volume are relatively useless as investment information.

Are there particular publications or types of articles that can educate you better than others? Are there commentators you can listen to who are trying to teach you something and who are not seeking to sell you a product? Is there any one piece of information you should try to glean from a daily market report?

I am going to conclude this chapter with a threefold listing of some suggested reading and watching aids. Each list builds on the one preceding it. Since I am giving actual names, please be aware the recommendations are my own based on my experience. They are not those of my firm or any other financial institution.

Beginning Investor: Low Interest, Little Time

Reading suggestions:

- business section in local newspaper
- business/financial section in *USA Today*
- money advice columns in magazines directed to a specific audience i.e., *Self, Working Woman, Modern Maturity*
- *Money* magazine
- your monthly or quarterly brokerage statement, mutual fund statement, credit union, bank, 401(k) updates, etc.
- research your broker sends you
- statement inserts from your brokerage house or mutual fund company

Viewing suggestions:
- weekend recap of business events on CNN
- online chat groups, special interest topics, business hot news.

Intermediate Investor: Medium Interest, Moderate Time

Reading suggestions:

- *Wall Street Journal/Investor's Business Daily/Individual Investor*—any newspaper like this for daily information
- *Business Week*—a weekly recap of domestic and international financial and business news—not of much value for investment ideas if not read on a timely basis
- business section of *Time, Newsweek, U.S. News & World Report*
- annual reports from the companies whose stock you own. Pay special attention to the president's or CEO's letter to shareholders for explanation of what went right/wrong during the year and for forecasts regarding the upcoming year. In the financial tables at the end of the report, note especially the balance sheet—you want to see more in current assets than current liabilities—and the income statement—net earnings, net income per share, comparison of these figures going back a few years.
- read your proxy and vote it
- quarterly reports from these same companies
- books and publications available from organizations such as AARP (American Association of Retired Persons) and OWL (Older Women's League).

Viewing (and listening) suggestions:

- CNBC—particularly at 8:30 A.M. for a view to that day's market activity or after 4:00 P.M. for a review and commentary on what did occur
- "Nightly Business Report"—National Public Television
- CNN's "Moneyline" (night)

- "Wall Street Week"
- talk programs that feature a person from the business or financial community
- National Public Radio "Marketplace" program
- videotapes that might be available from your brokerage firm or mutual fund company
- meeting of an investment club.

Experienced Investor: High Interest, Lots of Time

Reading suggestions:

- *Barron's, Forbes, Fortune, The Economist, Inc.*
- subscription newsletters from well-known market gurus and money managers—technical and fundamental (Stan Weinstein, Martin Sass, Mario Gabelli)
- special-interest journals and newsletters, such as *The Dow Theory, Value Line, Morningstar, Moody's Investors Services*
- utilize online investment information produced by America Online, CompuServe, Dow Jones market Monitor, Prodigy, and Reuters
- regional newspapers that give intensive coverage, e.g., *Crain's Chicago Business, San Jose Mercury Business*
- *Money Book Club.*

Participation suggestions:

- Take an adult education class at your local college, university, or extension program.
- Attend workshops, seminars, and lectures hosted by brokerage firms, mutual fund companies, accounting firms, newspaper publishers, planned giving organizations, etc.
- Check the bookshelves at the library and in bookstores for general finance information books or those directed to your special interests and gender.
- Put one of the morning or evening business programs on your everyday must-watch list.

19

Do Not Make These Investment Mistakes!

I CAN NOT GUARANTEE that every one of your stock purchases is going to go up. Nor can I promise that a bond you purchase will never lose its top credit rating or that it will not be called away from you prior to its expected maturity date. What I will say with complete assurance is that if you faithfully *avoid* the following list of investment traps, you will be giving your investment plan the best possible chance of success.

✔ *Do not believe there is one universally ideal investment.*
I mentioned earlier in the book that every woman wants to make money, to avoid losing money, and to avoid paying taxes. One of these features must predominate. Every woman also wants to find the one investment that is completely safe, pays a large dividend, and continues to rise in price. Likewise, she is going to have to decide which of these three features is the one she is going to concentrate on. I would be wary of any situation a broker tells you about that looks too perfect. That broker is going too hard for the sale. If you need income, you want to hear that the dividend payout is secure. If your goal is safety of principal, make sure you are looking at low-risk investments.

✔ *Do not panic over news events and call your broker with a reflex sell order.*
Catastrophic events do affect the stock market, but give the

market time to right itself before you make a hasty decision. Selling irrationally never serves a good purpose. It is more than likely you will regret your move within a few days and, meantime, you will have dealt your investment plan a bad blow. You may still decide to sell at a later time, but you and your broker will have made the decision together. You should expect to modify your plan. Economic or political events can signal that alteration. But make that change deliberately.

✔ *Do not buy hot tips—whether they be from a friend, your dentist, or the hot-shot commentators on television—without doing your own research.*

I'm not bad-mouthing tips in general. I have received my own share of good and lousy ones. Tips are high-risk investments, but if your portfolio has a place for this type of tool, check it out. And that is the point—checking it out. If you have a home PC and online capabilities, you can probably learn something all by yourself without even calling your broker. If not, call her and she can retrieve up-to-date information on her own computer. Leap if you want, but make sure you do some looking first.

✔ *Do not be afraid to take a loss.*

Some market theories say if a stock goes down 10 or 20 percent from your purchase price, you should automatically sell it. I personally do not recommend that thinking. The markets are too volatile these days. You could be out of a position just because of daily gyrations. In general, you sell a stock because its performance does not meet your expectations, it is no longer meeting your own objectives, your finances have changed, or the economy has dictated a change in your plan.

Conversely, some women become too attached to their stocks. Neither emotions nor ego should ever enter into an investment decision. Just because you once thought a certain stock, bond, or fund was the exact right one for you, that does not mean it is going to continue to be right. This works on the downside as well as on the upside. You have heard the expression "cut your losses." There does come a time when a stock is down and it is the right time to say good-bye. Move on to another investment that will serve you better.

✔ *Do not blame yourself—or your broker—unduly if an investment does not work out.*

Losses happen, and it is not necessarily your fault of your broker's. To look at the bright side of taking a loss, perhaps you have also taken gains during the year. Losses balance against gains dollar for dollar. One market strategy at year-end is to take enough losses to counter the realized gains. If you are still keen on the losing stock, you can buy it back after thirty-one days and you will have established a lower cost basis for yourself. The thirty-one-day waiting period involves what is called the wash sale rule. The loss on any security is not allowed if that same issue is bought back within thirty-one days.

✔ *Do not look for the one stock that will win back all the losses you took by selling the above loser.*

This statement is self-evident. You obviously do not like seeing your portfolio drop in value, but stick to your measured approach to investing. Looking for the killer stock or high income replacement could cause even more portfolio deterioration.

✔ *Do not be seduced by fancy products.*

Margin is to be used for a specific purpose—to use the benefit of its leverage if you need to "borrow" money for a short term period. Options and commodities will also have a limited use in your portfolio. They should be considered investment tools only for those women who have a very high risk-tolerance and can handle the loss.

Never use gimmicks, fads, or market derivatives to boost your portfolio value. The biggest and most sophisticated investors got burned. Learn the lesson from them and let your own hard-earned money continue to work for you in the traditional way.

✔ *Do not ignore changes in tax legislation.*

Changes in the tax code can impact your portfolio and its objectives. Stay current with these changes. For instance, if IRA contributions again become deductible to everyone, you will probably want to resume making those contributions. There is a great deal of talk going on about new favorable capital gains treatment. The holding period for stocks sold either at a loss or a gain would be affected. It is important that you review with your tax adviser your investment strategies and objectives in light of any tax savings and advantages.

✔ *Do not have unrealistic expectations.*

Time is money, but time is needed to make money, too. I said in the very beginning of this book that one of the elements of successful investing is patience. You need to give your investments the time they need to accomplish what you intend them to do. Just as there is a time to get out, there is also a time to stay in. The hot tip is expected to yield immediate gratification (or disappointment). The serious investment tool is not. It is bought for consistency and for the longer term. If you become un-disciplined in your actions, your portfolio is going to reflect the same unruly pattern.

20

Do Follow These Investing Principles

BUILDING WEALTH INVOLVES MUCH MORE than negative cautions. I prefer to end on an optimistic note. Let us finish our session by concentrating on what to do to make your investing as profitable and as pleasurable as possible.

What to do in investing is not the opposite of what not to do. The points in italics highlighting what to do in your investment framework are important to follow and remember in their own right.

✔ *Do set aside the amount designated as your investment money.*

Do not siphon away from other slices of the pie (which represent all your resources) in order to fund this area. Similarly, do not steal from this slice to make up for overindulgences in other areas.

✔ *Do review how you and your husband have divided up titles to all of your property.*

Consider again if you should set up any joint accounts with either a child or a potentially dependent parent.

✔ *Do talk to your lawyer and your accountant about the best IRA payout strategy for yourself.*

The decision you make by your first payout date will be the one you (and your heirs) will have to live and deal with from then on. This is also the logical time to make sure the beneficiary designated on any account is still the person you intend it to be.

✔*Do invest where you spend.*

I discussed this element of investing early in the book, but the advice bears repeating. Maybe you do your browsing at the local boutique bookstore but you do your buying at Barnes & Noble. For a getaway weekend, do you go to Atlantic City or to Disney World? Are the casinos busy? You might be interested in a gambling stock. Are there lines at Disney World? Don't forget Disney is a huge publicly owned company.

✔*Do emphasize diversification in your portfolio.*

A one-vision approach is self-destructive. Do think beyond owning only tax-free bonds. Try to avoid succumbing to the yearn for yield and investing solely in high-yield utility stocks. In your retirement years that is a normal reaction but you might be subjecting yourself either to the alternative minimum tax or to a loss in principal if interest rates take a big jump up.

✔ *Do avoid locked-in, illiquid investments.*

The lure of saving on taxes never goes away. The closer you are to retirement years, however, the less you should be buying investment tools that cannot be easily liquidated. Single premium life insurance products are appropriate for the early years, not for the later ones. During retirement you will be withdrawing from these annuities, not funding them. Some limited partnerships and direct investments hold the promise of capital gain or a high-income stream down the line. Investigate carefully before you buy, but *do* remember that these products rarely can be sold in the open market.

Do sell for the right reasons:

1. You lose faith in management. Management changes either in the officers of a company in which you have bought stock or by a portfolio manager in a mutual fund purchase signal a need for closer monitoring in the near term.
2. The stock or fund you own is the sole poor performer in that particular industry. Conversely, if your stock or fund is performing the best, you may want to add to your investment. Keep your winners and dump your losers.
3. Political or economic events are unfavorable. For example, import and export regulations are affecting performance; the dollar is weak against other currencies and you own stock in a company whose sales are concentrated abroad.
4. The stock or fund has given you the return you anticipated, and now it is time to look elsewhere. Or else, this particular investment has come to the end of its time period and you must withdraw the money—as with zero coupon bonds purchased for college education, for example.

✔ *As an investor, do keep your emotions in check.*

I spoke about the foolhardy attitude of becoming too attached to any one stock or fund. In addition, no investment is worth keeping if it has you awake at night or calling your broker every day for quotes. Get rid of it.

√ *Do plan with a goal. Do stick to that plan. Do make that plan a balanced one.*

You're confident about your well-diversified plan. You have spent the time necessary to design it to meet your own financial objectives, and you have determined what time periods are necessary to allow each of the investment tools to work best for you. You are not intending to short-circuit the system. Your goal is to let the sytem help you achieve your own financial goals. You have learned the lessons of this book well.

Conclusion

NATHAN ROTHSCHILD, one of the greatest money men of all time, said in 1834: "It requires a great deal of boldness, and a great deal of caution, to make a great fortune; and when you have got it, it requires ten times as much wit to keep it."

That is what this whole book is about—making and keeping money—in other words, investing. Investing insures that you plan, use, and increase your money.

These rules are the same for women as they are for men. A disproportionate number of women, however, have the double burden of not being trained in the market and admitting they are novices.

Beginning a financial awareness program is equivalent to starting a new fitness regime. It is never too late to become financially informed. Results will always occur as soon as you take the first steps.

Only 12 percent of women make the investment decisions in their households. That is because they say they do not know enough. This is frightening when statistics also indicate that 90 percent of all women will be responsible for their families' finances at some point in their lives.

The high-income woman may make over six figures a year. She may even have an advanced degree. What she does not have is any more preparation in dealing with financial realities than her compatriot at the low end of the earning scale. A woman's ability to make financial evaluations and to act on them relies on her exposure to investment information and her risk-toler-ance—not on her income level or her age.

I have built wealth for many of my clients. This book was written to help you do the same for yourself. Let this be your financial role model. Even though my case studies are of fictional women, let their experiences show you that you can do the same with your money as they did with theirs.

I know you have the confidence now to begin—or to modify—your investment planning. You should be comfortable with investment terms and strategies. If you find that you are still wary of asking your financial adviser a question, I would suggest you are with the wrong adviser. What should prove of more satisfaction to you, however, is that perhaps you can find your own answer by referring to the appropriate section in this book.

I sincerely hope that by now each woman, young or old, single or married, working or retired, is a believer in the value of investing. I encourage all of you to take the time now to ensure that your money is working for you in exactly the way you want it to. Be aware of your own money, your own temperament, and your own financial needs. Building wealth by investing successfully will be your reward.

Index

12b-1 Fund, 74
401(k) plans, 90–94, 104, 108, 109, 112, 119, 120, 124, 136, 138
403(b) plans, 94, 112
$125,000 exclusion, 124, 134, 142

Accumulation unit value, 99
Ages fifty-five and up, 131–46
    basic rules for, 145
    elderly or dependent parents and, 135
    estate planning and, 133
    examples for, 141–44
    goal setting for, 131
    IRA withdrawals for, 135–41
        examples, 141–44
    sale of homes and, 134, 142
Ages forty to fifty-four, 114–30
    examples for, 118–30
    protective devices and, 115–18
Ages twenty-five to thirty-nine, 103–13
    examples for, 104–13
Aggressive growth funds, 80
Alimony, 115–17, 141
American Exchange (AMEX), 39, 46, 80
America Online, 64
Annuities, tax-deferred, 96–102, 115–16
    fixed rate, 97–98
    variable, 98–101
Apple Computer, 45–46
Assets
    definition of, 9
    total, 14–15
    worksheet, 12, 15
AT&T stock, 128–29

Audit Investment Research Inc., 47

Back-end charge, 74
Balanced funds, 79–80
Banker's acceptance note, 29
Banks, working with, 68–70
Beginning investor, 152–53
Bond funds, 113
Bonds, 34–37, 143, 145
    coupons of, 31, 35
    deep discount, 51
    EE, 69
    high-yield (junk), 51
    lower-rated, 43–44
    rating of, 22, 35
    taxable vs. tax-free, 34
    Treasury, 30, 34
    zero coupon, 37, 110–12, 122, 125, 138
Bond mutual funds, 36, 81–82
Brokerage account, joint name, 116
Business Week, 73

Calls, 53
Capital gain, definition of, 76–77
Cash account, 52, 54
Certificates of deposit (CDs), 29–30, 104, 105, 118–20, 119–20
Charles Schwab, 64
Child support, 115, 117, 127
Closed-end funds, 71–72
Collectibles, 55–56
Commercial paper, 29
Commodities trading (futures contracts), 54
Common stock, 35, 38–39
Country funds, 80
Coupons, bond, 31, 35

Custodian accounts, 110–12, 127, 135

Deep discount bonds, 51
Discount brokers, 63–64
Diversification, 21, 45, 73, 127–28, 146, 160
Divorce, 115–18, 141
Dollar-cost averaging, 106
Domestic stock funds, 79
Dreyfus Intermediate Municipal Bond, 36–37

EE bonds, 69
Emerging-country stock, 51
Emerging-growth stock, 51
Emerging market funds, 82–83
Estate planning, 115–16, 133
E Trade, 64
Experienced investor, 154–55

FDIC (Federal Deposit Insurance Corp.), 78
Federal Farm Credit Bureau, 34
Federal Home Loan Bank, 34
Federal Reserve Bank, 31
Federal Reserve Board, 32, 52
Fidelity Emerging Markets, 83
Fidelity Investments, 64, 71, 74–75, 100
Fidelity Limited Term Municipals, 36
Financial planning, 115
Fixed-rate annuity, 97–98
Forbes magazine, 73
Front-end funds, 74
Full-service brokerage house, 58–63
Fundamental data bases, 149–50
Futures contract. *See* Commodities trading (futures contracts)

Global bond funds, 82
Global stock funds, 80–81
Gold, 54–55
Growth and income funds, 79
Growth funds, 79
    aggressive, 80
Growth stocks, 44–46, 120, 137, 138, 143

Hartford Life, 100
High-risk funds, 82–83
High-risk investments, 41–48
    growth stocks, 44–46
    lower-rated bonds, 43–44
    real estate investment trusts (REITS), 46–47
High-yield bonds (junk bonds), 51
Homes, sale of, 124–25, 134, 142

Ibbotson & Associates, 20–21
Illiquid investments, avoiding, 160
Individual Retirement Accounts (IRAs), 85–89, 120–24, 125–27
    withdrawals from, 139–41, 160
    withdrawing from, 135–41
Initial public offerings (IPOs), 51–52
Interest rates, 150, 151
Intermediate investor, 153–54
International or foreign funds, 80
Investing
    about, 1–5
    alternatives for, 24. *See also specific investments*
    definition of, 1
    goal setting for, 17–19
    principles of, 159–61
    reasons for, 6–8
Investment clubs, 148
Investment mistakes, 155–58
Investment money, 9–16, 159. *See also* Personal financial profile
IRAs. *See* Individual Retirement Accounts (IRAs)

Joint accounts, 159
Joint ownership, 115–16
Joint Tenant With Right of Survivorship (JTWROS), 116, 124
Junk bond funds, 81–82
Junk bonds, 51

Keogh plans, 89, 90, 121, 125, 136, 142

Liabilities
    definition of, 9

Liabilities (*cont'd.*)
  total, 14–15
  worksheet, 13–14
Life expectancy, IRA withdrawals and, 139–41
Lincoln National Life, 100
Living expenses worksheet, 10–12, 15
Living trust, 133
Load fund, 74
Lower-rated bonds, 43–44
Low-risk investments, 26–32
  certificates of deposit (CDs), 29–30, 119–20
  money market accounts, 28–29
  passbook savings accounts, 28
  Treasury bills, 30–32
Lynch, Peter, 71

Magellan Fund, 71
Margin account, 52, 54
Marital deduction, 116
Medium-risk investments, 33–40
  bonds, 34–37
  stock
    common, 38–39
    preferred, 37–38
Metals, precious, 54–55
Money funds, 78–81
Money market accounts, 28–29, 108–9
Money-purchase pension plan, 89
Montgomery Emerging Markets, 83
Moody's, 22, 35, 81
Morningstar, 73, 74, 77, 100
Municipal bond funds, 81
Muriel Siebert & Co., 64
Mutual funds, 71–84
  benefits of, 71–72
  brokerage vs. fund companies, 75–77
  classification of, 73–74
  closed-end, 71–72
  definition of, 36
  literature of, 74–75
  open-end, 71, 72
  selection of, 77–84
    bonds, 81–82

high risk, 82–83
  money funds, 78–81
  unit investment trusts, 71, 72

National Association of Securities Dealers Automated Quotron (NASDAQ), 39, 45–46
Net asset value (NAV), 72, 73, 75, 76
Net worth, 9, 15
New York Stock Exchange (NYSE), 39, 46, 51, 52, 80
Nightly Business Report, 118, 147, 151
No-load fund, 73
Nuveen New York, 112

Oil prices, 150, 151
Open-end funds, 71, 72
Options, 53–54

Parents, support of, 117–18, 135
Participation suggestions, 154–55
Passbook savings accounts, 28
Penny stock, 52
Personal financial profile, 9–16
  assets and, 12, 15
  liabilities and, 13–14
  living expenses worksheet and, 10–12, 15
Preferred stocks, 35, 37–38
Probate, 133
Profit-sharing plan, 89
Puts, 53

Quick & Reilly Inc., 64

Reading suggestions, 152–54
Real estate investment trusts (REITS), 46–47
Recalculation method, 140
Record keeping, 145
Regional funds, 80
Regulated investment company. *See also* Mutual funds
  definition of, 71
Retirement plans, 85–95
  401(k) plans, 90–94, 104, 108, 109, 112, 119, 120, 124, 138

403(b) plans, 94, 112
for ages forty to fifty-four, 118–30
for ages twenty-five to thirty-nine,
107–9, 112
bank, 68–69
Individual Retirement Accounts
(IRAs), 85–89, 120–24, 125–27
Keogh plan, 121, 125
Keogh plans, 89, 90
simplified employee pensions
(SEPs), 90
Risk-tolerance, 20–25
quiz on, 23–24
Robert A. Stanger and Co., 47
Rothschild, Nathan, 162

Savings account. *See* Passbook
savings accounts
Scudder, 100
Sector funds, 82
Securities and Exchange
Commission (SEC), 75
Selling, right reasons for, 161
Simplified employee pensions
(SEPs), 90
Speculative investments, 49–57
collectibles, 55–56
commodities trading (futures
contract), 54
definition of, 51
emerging-country stock, 51
emerging-growth stock, 51
high-yield bonds (junk bonds), 51
initial public offerings (IPOs),
51–52
margin account, 52, 54
options, 53–54
penny stock, 52
precious metals, 54–55
venture real estate, 54
Standard & Poor's, 22, 35, 81
Standard & Poor's 500 Index, 21, 22,
53
Standard & Poor's Lipper Mutual
Fund Profiles, 77
Stock, 5, 128–29, 143
common, 35, 38–39

emerging-country, 51
emerging-growth, 51
growth, 44–46, 120, 137, 138, 143
option, 53–54
penny, 52
preferred, 35, 37–38
rating of, 22
Stockbrokers, 58–67
discount, 63–64
firing of, 66–67
full-service, 58–63
Stock funds
domestic, 79
global, 80–81
Stock market, 1987 crash of, 3

Taxable bond funds, 81
Taxable bonds, 34
Taxable money funds, 78
Tax-deferred annuities. *See* Annuities,
tax-deferred
Taxes, 146
estate planning and, 116, 133
home sales and, 124, 134–35
IRA withdrawals and, 135–44
Tax-free bonds, 34
Tax-free or tax-advantaged money
funds, 78–79
Technical data bases, 149–50
Term certain, 140–41
The Travelers, 100
Time Warner stock, 119, 120
Treasury bills, U.S. (T-bills), 21, 29,
30–32, 129
Treasury bonds, 30, 34
Trusts
for grandchildren, 145
living, 133

Uniform Gifts to Minors Act (UGMA),
110–11
Unit investment trusts, 71, 72

Value Line, 77
Vanguard, 100
Vanguard International Index-
Emerging, 83

Vanguard Municipal Bond Fund
    Intermediate, 37
VARDS Report, 100
Variable annuity, 98–101
Venture real estate, 54
Viewing suggestions, 153–54

Wills, 115, 116, 133

Yankelovich, 118

Zero coupon bonds, 37, 110–12, 122,
    125, 138